Debunkum Beaver
Pega How-to Guide

Creating REST Service and REST Connector
(How-to Version)

Copyright Notice

Disclaimer

*The content within the publication is based solely on the
author's personal knowledge and experiences, and it does not represent any
other entities' views, either directly, or implied.*

*Readers' should view this publication as another point of view,
use it as a reference and sought their own conclusion.*

*Although the author and publisher
have made every effort to ensure that the
information in this book was correct at time of print,
the author and publisher do not assume and hereby disclaim any
liability to any party for any loss, damage, or disruption
caused by errors or omissions, whether such
errors or omissions result from
negligence, accident, or any
other causes.*

*The information in this book
is meant to supplement, not replace Pega Academy trainings.
Readers should ensure that they have completed the relevant Pega courses,
and to consult Pega Academy on matters related
to their trainings or certifications.*

*This is a non-official guide, and it is
created as a form of knowledge sharing, and presented as it is
without any warranties. Usage is entirely
at the reader's own risk.*

*By reading and using information in this
book, you signified your acceptance of these and assume all
responsibilities for its usage.*

Dedication & Acknowledgements

First of all, I think we all need to thank
Alan Trefler, without him, there would not be the Pega
we are seeing today. It is also him, who kept Pega as a free company,
which was evident in the Reuters article on 'rather
eat sand than sell to other companies'.
Hopefully, Pega will continue
to be independent.

Special thanks to my dear wife
for the support provided for me to achieve
the CLSA certification, as well as the sacrificed family time
and encouragement she had provided me with to leverage on my academic
knowledge to contribute back to the community through this book.
Not to forget my boy, who volunteered to create a logo for
Debunkum Beaver, at the same time,
being my proof reader!

There were multiple great
SSAs/LSAs along my journey, who had
explained many important Pega concepts and guided
me in the past years. Their untiring explanations
and demonstrations are
greatly appreciated.

This book is a
dedication to all those who
would like to embark on the Pega Learning Journey.
With this, you now have one more
reliable resource.

Contents

Who Is This Book For?

This Guide: **Debunkum Beaver Pega How-to Guide** is a series for everyone, people who are new to Pega as well as those who are experienced in Pega.

The prerequisite is just to have some basic understanding of Pega, preferably to have at least completed the Pega CSA training.

Being certified in Pega is not required, but a keen desire to learn Pega is a must!

Preface

Thanks for purchasing Debunkum Beaver Pega How-to Guide! In order to fully maximise the book, it is important to understand the purposes and positioning of this How-to series.

Why Create a Pega How-to Guide?

Strictly speaking, information on Pega "how-to" can be found in Pega Community, Pega Academy, as well as throughout the Internet.

Even if the information is not readily available, all that is needed is simply to create a new Pega Community post; and somehow, after some time, there would be people from the community, Pega GCS or even Pega Engineering, jumping in to provide the answer, so isn't such a how-to guide unnecessary?

Well, technically, you could argue it in that way. However, in all engagements, one of the most challenging things is "deadline". Often, a go-live date would be defined well before requirement specification was even signed off.

Therefore, there is basically no time to search for information, wait for replies, or learn and explore how to implement certain features/requirements in an actual project scenario – at the very moment when it is required.

Apart from that, the replies from various sites are often not an end-to-end, step-by-step guide, that are complete with screenshots; worse, those would not include validation and testing steps.

Therefore, it would require prior Pega knowledge and additional effort to clarify, test and finally implement it.

To make matter worse, can you imagine the additional stress that you are subjected to when you thought that you had the solution, but after much testing and trying, it doesn't work!!!

To add on to the challenges, the profile of the team members often creates another dimension of issues. This problem has 2 extremities:

1) **<u>New Users of Pega:</u>** Those who are totally new to Pega
2) **<u>Senior and Experienced Pega SSA/LSA:</u>** Those who have many years of experiences, some even spanned across Pega V5.x and V6.x

For New Users of Pega, they do not know how to implement a lot of things in Pega, thus a lot of hand-holding and samples are required to guide them along and get them to be efficient.

There is technically not much issues with them, just the need to provide them with some relevant examples, or even implement one instance of the solution, explain to them how it works, and they would be able to get started and replicate the implementation across other parts of the application.

The downside is that a lot of time is required to create relevant samples and to help them in debugging issues that may occur.

On the other hand, Senior and Experienced Pega SSAs/LSAs, although are self-starters and able to start implementation without much guidance, they introduced another kind of problem – their solutions to all problems are often "activities" and "agents"!!!

> *Note: These are the groups that I am most wary of. They know enough to create devastating calamities. Their 'pride' often led them to position themselves as the 'centre-of-the-universe' and the reluctance to listen. Getting good people from this group, who are open to ideas, willing to listen and integrate the overall Pega solution into the enterprise is like searching for a needle in a haystack. I have written a separate chapter on this in the How-to Guide, read through to understand how to source for a good Pega resource for your next project!*

Any other issues that cropped up along the way, would often be yet another activity, custom Java codes or some HTML, JavaScripts; the worst that I have seen, was creating multiple Boolean variables to cater for various flows and decisions throughout the whole application for handle difference scenario and business changes!!!

With all those Boolean variables, in order to understand the whole logic (and ensure it is correct), you need to kept track of all the Boolean variables that are set/unset throughout all the activities, data transforms, flows, UIs, button clicked, etc.! Isn't that a BIG pain? How could the application ever be reliable?

Technically, they can implement the required features, but whatever they had touched, can no longer be easily modified by another SSA/LSA without the corresponding number of years of experience, not to mention about the underlying performance and maintenance issues that were introduced!

In view of all these challenges, Debunkum Beaver has decided to embark on this path: A How-to Guide for Pega.

For New Users of Pega, this series provide a step-by-step guide to implement any given feature; for Senior and Experienced Pega SSAs/LSAs, this guide shows the best practices and a standardised way of implementing the intended features, leveraging on the newer Pega capabilities to simplify the implementation, as much as possible.

With the Debunkum Beaver Pega How-to Guide series, you would have an arsenal of tools at your disposal. Whenever there is a new project, or a new feature required, all you have to do is just to pull out one of these guides. Cool right?

Can you visualise a situation, where all similar features have the same way of implementation, with the same sequence of steps and number of rules; and anyone who looked at the rules knew exactly how and why each rule was implemented as such; any deviations and bugs that were introduced due to carelessness would simply stand out by itself, easily identifiable and easy to fix, wouldn't this be a wonderful Pega World?

Well, that is the core objective of the **Debunkum Beaver Pega How-to Guide** series!

With the direction set, the next question is: "How Should I Categorise the Pega How-to Guide?"

How Should I Categorise the Pega How-to Guide?

Given that there are so many features, I couldn't just write <u>ONE book</u>, it would take ages, and by then, a new Pega version would be released!

Of course, I could potentially do a high-level grouping, e.g. *Pega Integration*, *Pega Reporting*, *Pega Case Management*, etc...

But there is one big problem...

Take *Pega Integration* as an example, there are so many types of integrations: SOAP, REST, OAuth2, etc. Does that mean that I should write all the integrations before publishing the *"Pega Integration"* book?

That would also take a long time, increase the overall price of the book and force readers to pay for things they don't need or are not interested in; worst, it would just end up as another version of Pega help file.

On top of that, if one of the integration methods changed, do I need to update the whole book as a new version?

Apart from the above issues, you may have realised another problem: I have not mentioned about another dimension of Integration: "*Service Packages* vs *Service Connectors*"!

So, should I have a book on *Pega Integration Service Connectors* and another on *Pega Integration Service Packages*? But I cannot separate them because I need to use the *Service Connectors* to invoke the *Service Packages* to test!

As you can see, things just get more and more messy...

I shared my problem with my boy, and asked him what books he enjoyed the most, and this is what he showed me - His private Mr Men Collection!

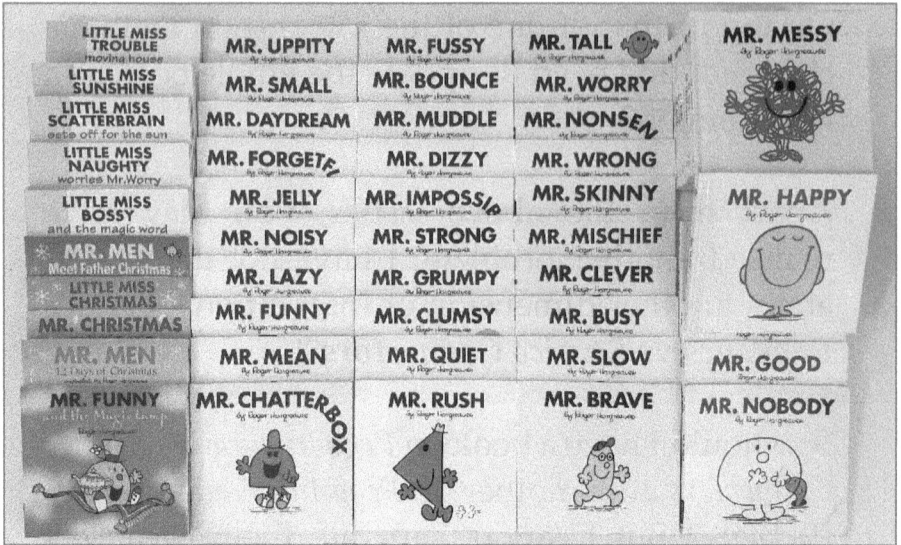

Figure 1: Mr Men Collection

He went on to explain how much he enjoyed the book. Although each single book is short, it is concise, and he can easily look for any Mr Men he wants; at the same time, priding himself as *"Mr Happy"*...

Well, although I felt that *"Mr Messy"* is a better match for him, I agree on his concept: *"Small little book that is concise, and easy to be used as a reference"*!

Yes! That is exactly how the *"Debunkum Beaver Pega How-to Guide"* would be released!

The next question is: How should I organise each Pega How-to Guide, so that it would achieve the core objective?

How Should I Organise Each How-to Guide?

I want to have a how-to guide suitable for both beginners and experts, one that could be used as a quick reference, yet without the unnecessary theories and documentation.

Yes, this is really a tall order, but anything less than that would not serve the purpose and would just end up being another Pega Community post or simply an excerpt of the Pega help file!

It must be able to provide something like a 2-mins run-through to illustrate the purpose and concept, like the typical *"Hello World!"* of programming, yet able to be expanded further into more useful stuff!

So here, *"Debunkum Beaver Pega How-to Guide"* is born! It sets out to achieve the above by applying the following:

1) Quick explanation of the purpose of the feature
2) A quick implementation using the typical *"Hello World"* style, demonstrating the feature in the simplest form
3) Expansion of the example using various scenario and extension of the features to cover related areas

In order to provide a quick explanation and make understanding of Pega concepts a breeze, at times, I might "state" that a given Pega feature is equivalent to something that is more commonly understood, followed by a series of scenario that further extend its capabilities and enable users to slowly appreciate the differences.

For example, I might start by stating: *"Think of Pega Data classes as Database tables..."*, and then proceeded with some scenario on how to use Pega Data Classes to add, update and delete records, followed by other interesting features, that would extend it capability and moved beyond just database tables. So, take note of this unique approach in the guide.

Versions of Pega How-To Guide

In order to launch the book fast and to keep cost down, as well as to contribute to the overall Pega community knowledge, the Pega How-to Guide will be released in 3 versions:

1) **Online Version:** This is a free version, published at *"DebunkumBeaver.com"*. Basically, selected chapters are published and contained all the information required to implement the intended feature. The details and quality of the instructions would often exceed those that are freely available on the Internet.

2) **How-to Version**: This version contains all the detailed steps, including complete screenshots on how to implement the intended feature. You can be sure that it would DEFINITELY work, because I would simplify the steps, actually do it from

scratch. Anything lesser than that would not meet the earlier set out objectives, agree?

3) **Master Beaver Version**: This version contains everything of the How-to Version, with the inclusion of analysis and the motivations for doing the given steps, as well as special scenario and limitations of the feature.

Which Version Should I Get?

Online Version

If you are an experienced Pega architect and just need some pointers and have the time to investigate and try out the details, this version suits your needs.

By comparing this version with the How-to version, you will be able to better appreciate my purpose of creating the Pega How-to Guide series, as well as its value.

How-to Version

This version is for people who just want to implement the basic feature in the quickest possible way. This version takes the readers through a step-by-step procedure, with complete screenshots, thus suitable for new users of Pega, who want to learn how to implement various features in Pega. The focus of this version is mainly on implementing the feature, explanation is kept to a minimum so as to enable a fast and efficient implementation.

Master Beaver Edition

If you are looking for more in-depth discussion, understand how and why the given feature was done in that way. This version is for you.

Most importantly, if you are considering taking Pega CLSA certification, it is always better to get the Master Beaver Version.

Author's Profile

The author is a Pega CLSA, certified in the new Pega CLSA Path (7.3/7.4). Academically, he has a master's degree and has experiences in teaching undergraduates pursuing master's and bachelor's degrees in World renowned universities.

Combining the above with his over 20 years of IT experiences in various MNCs, the author decided to write this series of Pega How-to Guide to help aspiring system architects to implement Pega in a faster, cleaner and more efficient way.

Why Not Do This At Pega Community?

This is an interesting option that I had considered before. However, there are a few stoppers:

Limited and Lack of Control

I hate the feeling of being restricted. I have many ideas, plans and ways of doing things, but when there are people or situations that restrict or delay me, I get very pissed off.

Lack of Details

Pega Community is good but more often than not, the replies are just one-liner, links to other articles, and a bunch of descriptions and steps, which would not help if you do not have good Pega knowledge in the first place. Interestingly, if you had that, you wouldn't need to go there to search for answers in the first place!

Do take note that I am not saying that Pega Community does not provide good information or solutions, it is just that it was not meant to teach and guide you like what you were taught in your undergraduate studies.

I Want To Teach and Have Students Who Want to Learn

The platform today, and possibly many years into the future, focuses on the technicality of how to do a task, not about the purpose, or the thought process that led to the solution, which is a crucial skill you would want to acquire if you want to pass the exams.

I needed a platform to allow me to do that, but in Pega Community, people have a stronger tendency to listen only to those 'renowned professional', who sometimes went down the 'too technical' path.

Therefore, there is basically no avenue that I could share the detailed and vast knowledge that I have.

Since I am an author, have the academic background, as well as a Pega CLSA, it makes perfect sense for me to do it through publications, thus, the birth of this book.

I want to teach, and if you want to learn, then welcome to the mind-blowing world of Debunkum Beaver!

Introduction

I am sure most, if not all of you, know about REST. REST stands for *"Representational State Transfer"*, it is a software architectural style that defines a set of constraints to be used for creating Web services.

In this How-to Guide, I will demonstrate how to use Pega to create REST service as well as REST connector. In a nutshell, REST service provides the service, while REST connector, as a client, consumes it.

REST/JSON is gaining traction, both for its ease of implementation as well as for its ease of consumption.

I am not going to do any academic definition, comparison with SOAP, etc, because you can easier get that information from the Internet.

Approach Used for This Guide

To facilitate ease of understanding, I shall start out with a minimalistic example – The familiar *"Hello World"* example.

After that, I shall make incremental changes so that it would become something more useful.

> *Note: This guide is based on Pega 7.4. If you are using earlier versions, you might not be able to perform certain functions, especially those newly added capabilities. If you are using Pega 8.x, please note that there is quite a number of changes, especially to the 'Designer Studio', for example, your login icon would be located on the bottom-left instead.*

Part 1: Completing the Groundwork

Create A New Application

If you would like some help on creating a new application and test users, this and the following chapters would be useful to you.

> 💡 _Note:_ _If you are an experience Pega user, you can just skip the groundwork section and jump straight to the REST Service section itself._

Login as a user who has the rights to create application, e.g. `administrator@pega.com` (default pwd is `install`). Click on the following menu item: _Application:XXX > New Application_

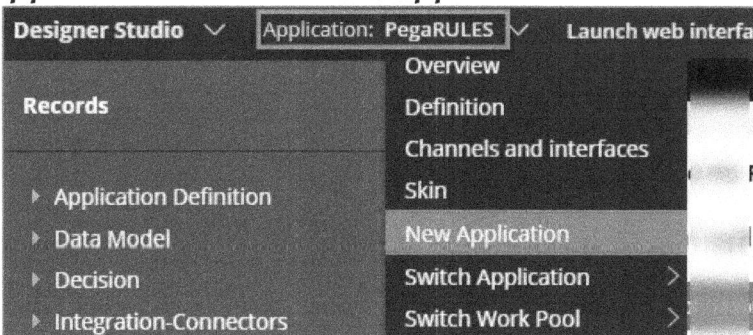

Designer Studio ∨	Application: PegaRULES ∨	Launch web interfa
	Overview	
Records	Definition	
	Channels and interfaces	
▸ Application Definition	Skin	
▸ Data Model	New Application	
▸ Decision	Switch Application >	
▸ Integration-Connectors	Switch Work Pool >	

Figure 2: Creating a New Application

> 💡 **Note:** *Don't worry about the "PegaRULES" on the right side of the "Application:" as shown in the diagram. By default, that shows the application that you are currently in, which does not really matter when you are just creating a new application.*

In the form that opens, click on the *"Custom"* as shown below:

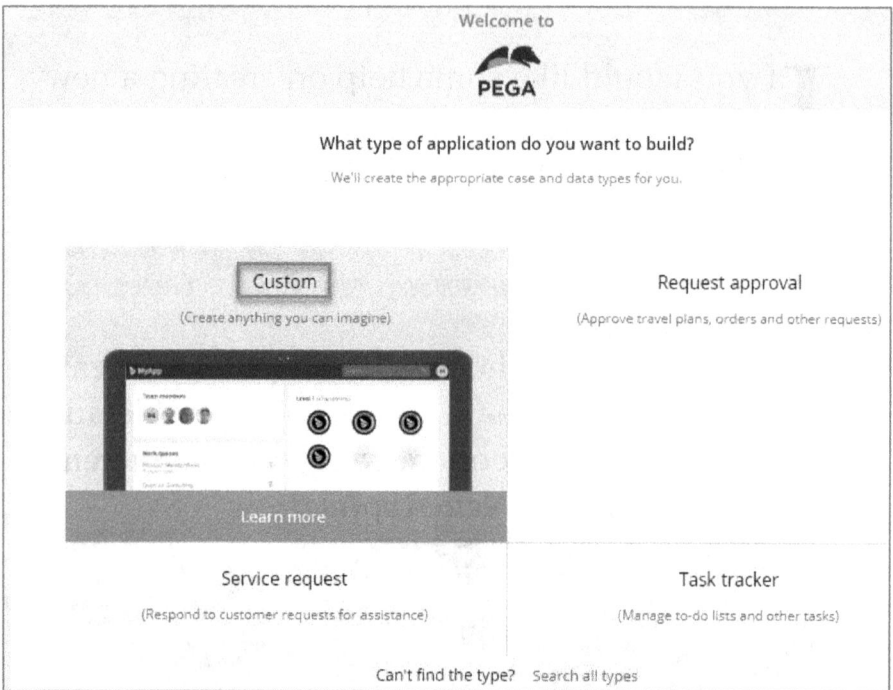

Figure 3: Creating a Custom Application

Click on the *"Use this application type"* to proceed.

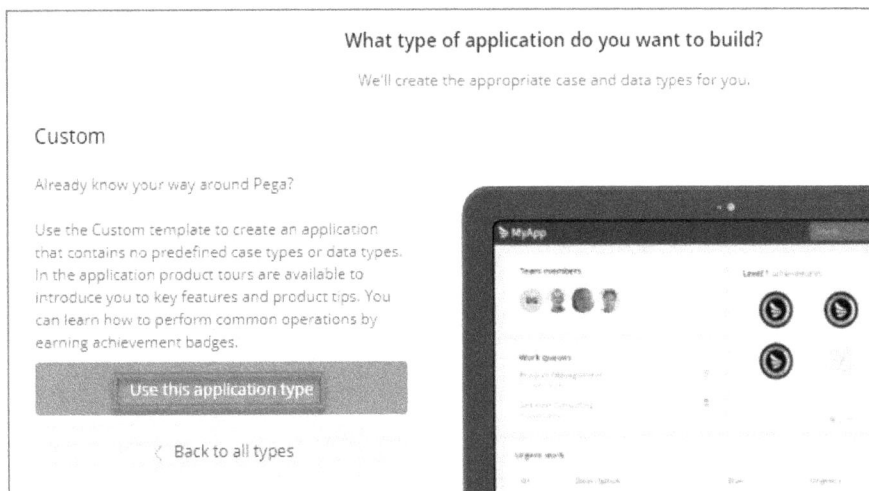

What type of application do you want to build?

We'll create the appropriate case and data types for you.

Custom

Already know your way around Pega?

Use the Custom template to create an application that contains no predefined case types or data types. In the application product tours are available to introduce you to key features and product tips. You can learn how to perform common operations by earning achievement badges.

Use this application type

‹ Back to all types

Figure 4: Confirming the Application Type

For the primary device, select *"Responsive"* as shown below:

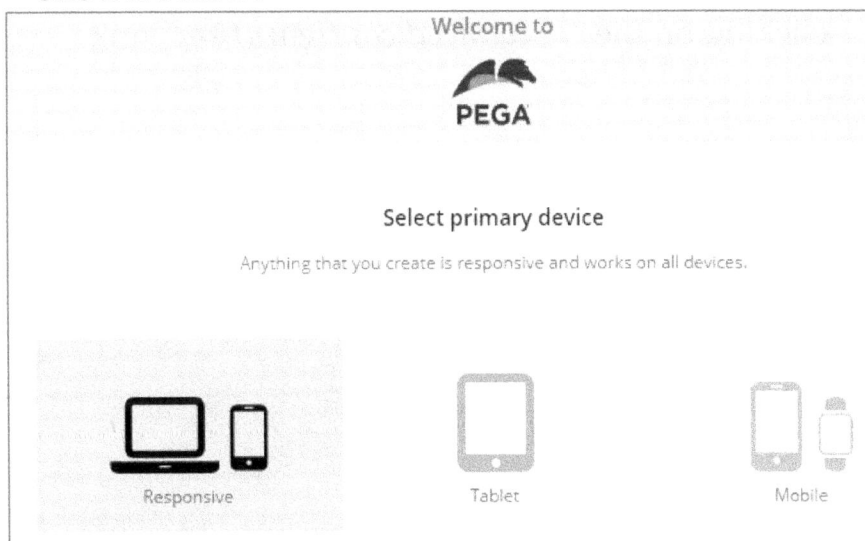

Welcome to

PEGA

Select primary device

Anything that you create is responsive and works on all devices.

Responsive   Tablet   Mobile

Figure 5: Selecting Responsive as the Primary Device

For the colour scheme, just choose the "*Default*".

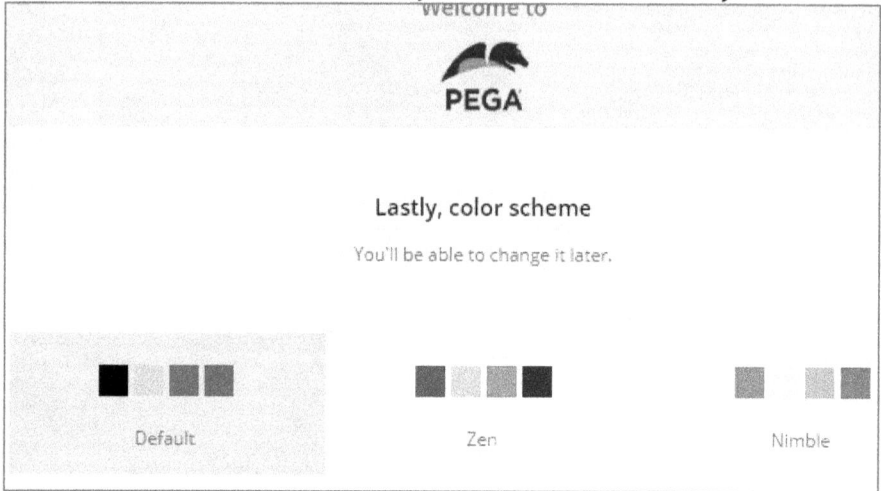

Figure 6: Selecting the Default Colour Scheme

Name your application as: "*DBRest*", followed by clicking on the "*Advanced configuration*" link.

> **Note:** *The following diagram shows the "ExpXLS" application as an example, you should name it according to the name given above.*

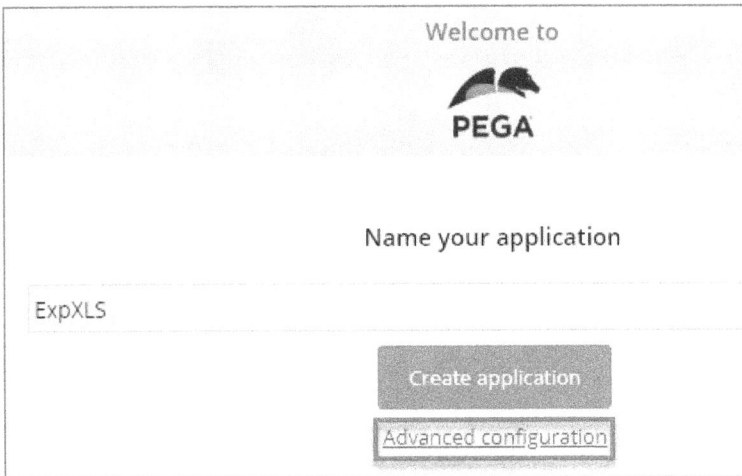

Figure 7: Sample of Application Name Screen for ExpXLS Application

In the *"Advanced configuration"* dialog shown below, ensure the following:

- Application structure: *Implementation*
- Application id: *DBRest*
- Organization name: *DB*
- Application: *DBRest*

The following is an example of the configuration.

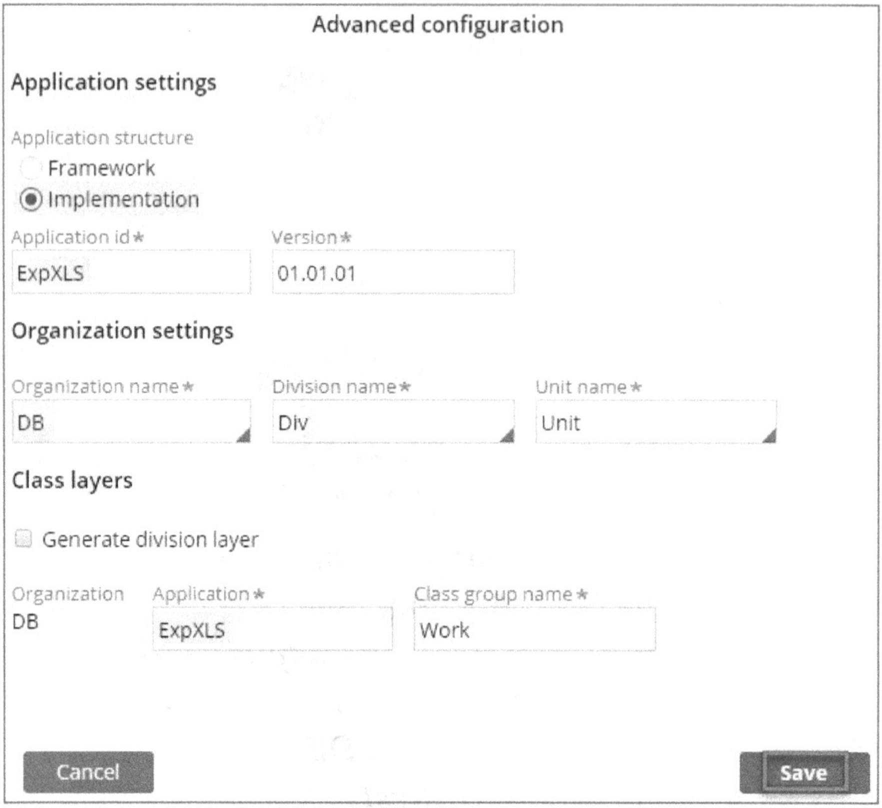

Figure 8: Sample of Advanced Configuration for ExpXLS Application

Click on the Save button to continue.

> Note: *If you are a new user of Pega, please follow exactly as above to avoid any problems (in this case, please use "DBRest"). The details of these settings are out of the scope of this book.*

You will now be brought back to the *"Name your application"* page, as shown below. Click on the *"Create application"* to create it.

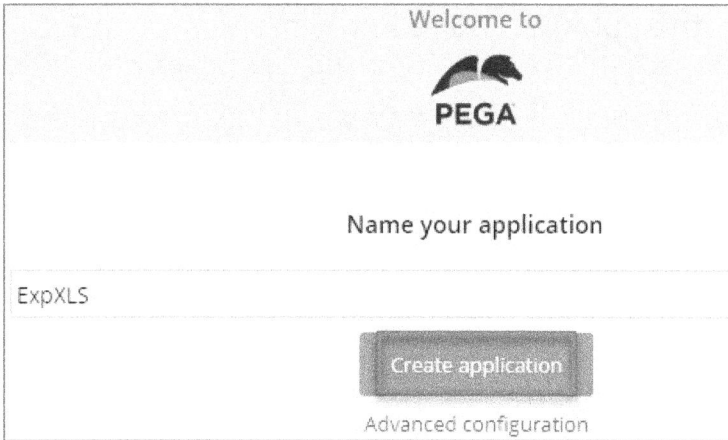

Figure 9: Example of Creating the ExpXLS Application

Once your application had been created, you will see the following confirmation:

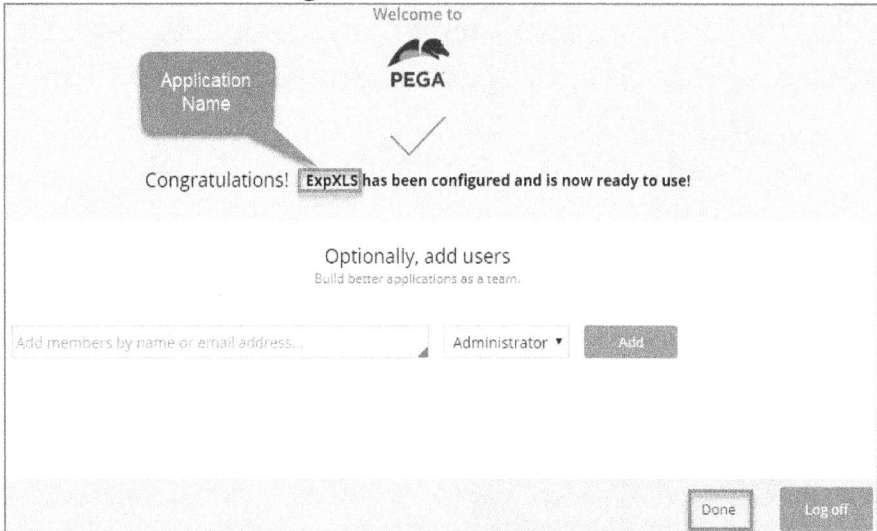

Figure 10: Example for the Confirmation of ExpXLS Application Creation

At this point, you could create new users by entering the name or email address. However, we shall not do it this way as it had assumed that many settings are already configured in the existing system, such as existing users, email server settings, etc.

Therefore, let's just click on the *"Done"* button to close this dialog box.

> **Note:** *In earlier versions of Pega, sample users are created. This is no longer the case in Pega 7.4.*

To validate that your application is created, click on the *"Records Explorer(1)"*, in the opened menu, under the *"Application Definition"*, click the *"Application(2)"*. You will now be able to see your newly created application on the right as shown below.

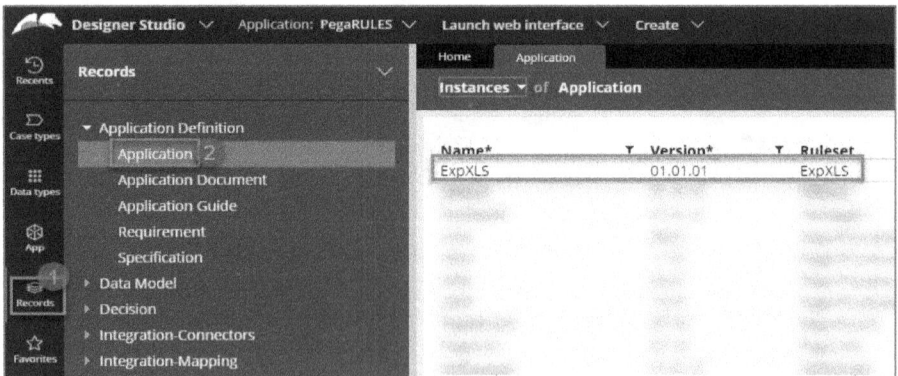

Figure 11: Example of Validating that ExpXLS Application Is Created

Apart from the application, you should also validate that your Access Groups are also created. In the "Records Explorer(1)", under "Security(2)", click the "Access Group(3)" menu item as shown below:

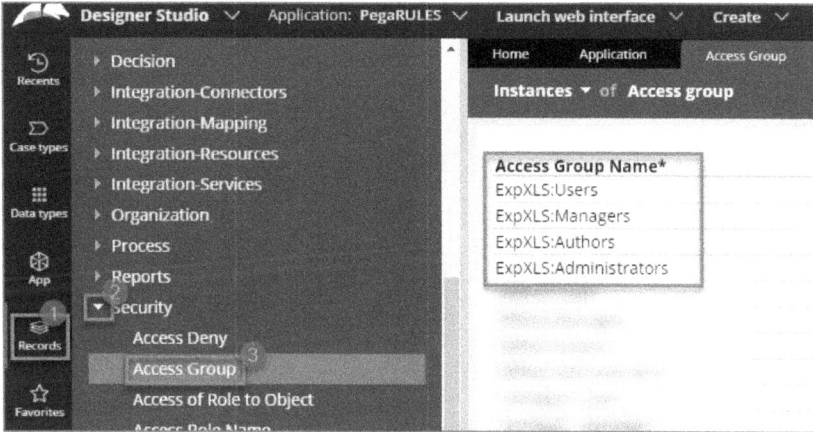

Figure 12: Example of Validating that ExpXLS Access Groups Are Created

You should see 4 Access Groups related to your application being created. The above is an example for the ExpXLS application.

Create Sample Test User

Next, we shall create a sample test user to facilitate demonstration and testing. The user will be named *"DBeaver"*, who is the administrator of the application.

For simplicity, we will also use the same user in other Pega How-to Guides.

If you had already created this user, you do not need to create it again, however, you would still need to assign the new access group of the application to this user.

Instructions for creating a new user, as well as granting existing user access to the new application are shown below, please follow the steps in the relevant section.

Creating New Users for The Application

This section explains how to create new users for a given application.

> **Note:** *If you would like to use an existing user instead of creating a new one, please skip this section and go to the next section, which provides details on how to grant existing user with access to your new application.*

To create new users, follow these steps:
1) Click on *"Records Explorer"*
2) Look for *"Organization"* and click its arrow on the left to expand it
3) Right-click on the *"Operator ID"*
4) On the context menu that pops up, click on the *"Create"*

The following diagram illustrates the steps:

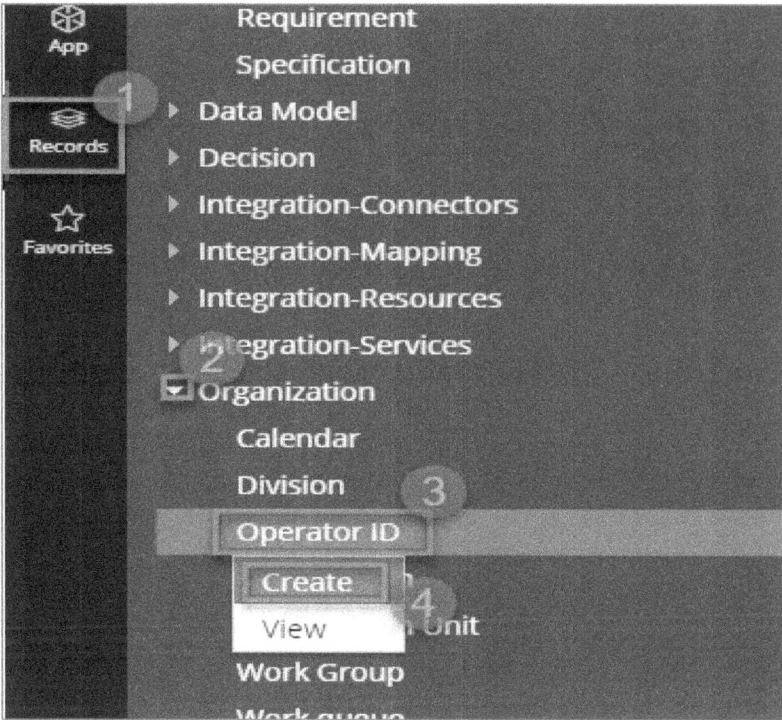

Figure 13: Creating a New Operator ID

On the create form, enter *"DBeaver"* for both the fields shown below, followed by clicking the *"Create and open"* button:

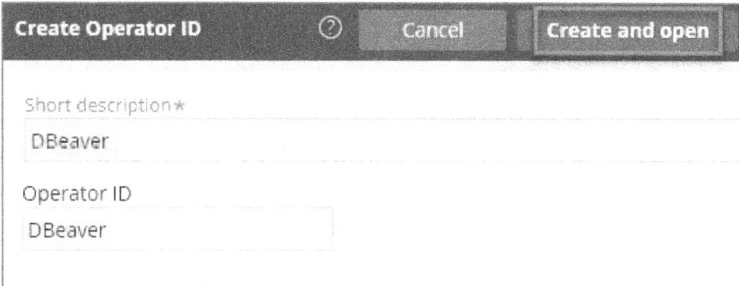

Figure 14: Creating Operator ID

With the DBeaver Operator ID opened, under the **"Profile"** tab, set the access group as *"DBRest:Administrators"*.

> ♀ **Note:** *If you did not use the "DBRest" as the application name earlier, you might need to replace the "DBRest:"with whatever application name you have created instead.*

The following screen shows a sample of the Profile tab.

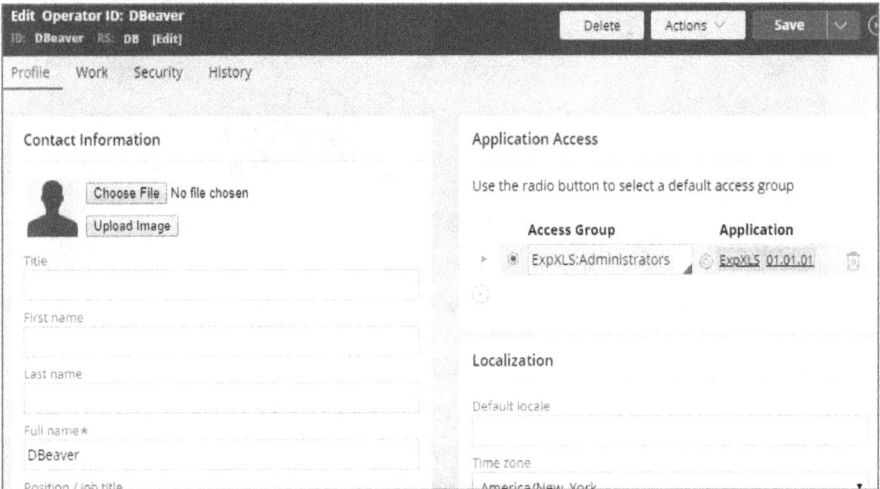

Figure 15: Sample of DBeaver With ExpXLS:Administrators Access Group

> ♀ **Note:** *Just a reminder: the above screenshot was for "ExpXLS" application. If you had created your application as "DBRest", you need to ensure that it is reflected accordingly above.*

Click on the *"Security"* tab, followed by clicking on the *"Update password"* button.

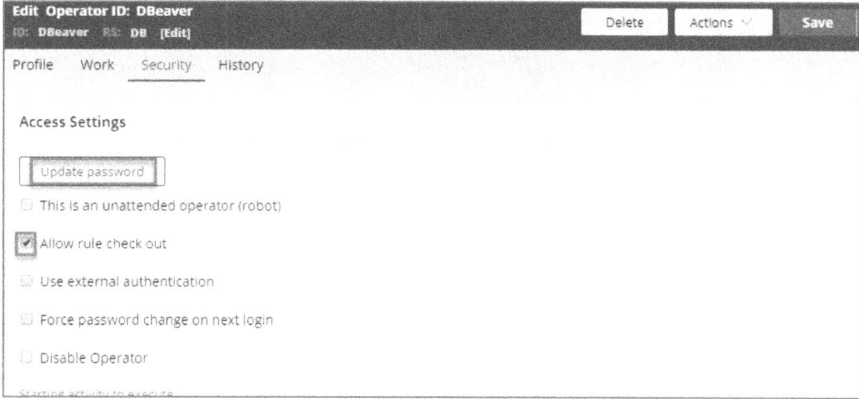

Figure 16: Sample of DBeaver Access Settings

In the dialog that popup as shown below:

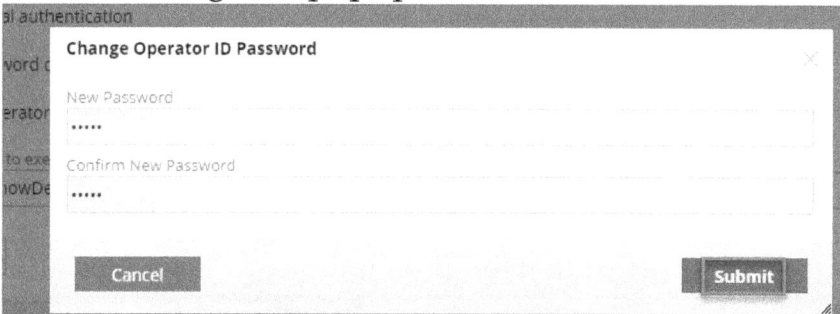

Figure 17: Changing Operator ID Password

Enter "*rules*" for both the highlighted fields above. After that, click the "*Submit*" button.

> **Note**: *Changing the password to [rules] is solely for convenience and demonstration purposes. If you are not able to use this simple password, it is likely that there are some password policies enforcing this. In such a case, the simplest way is to choose a more complex password that adhere to the policy. Please remember the password!*

Back in the *"Security"* tab, optionally, you may tick the *"Allow rule check out"* if you desired.

As a best practice, it is always better to enter some documentation in the *"History"* tab, as shown below.

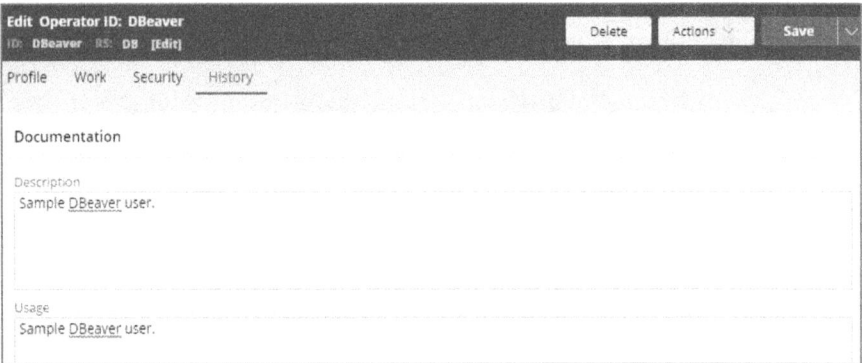

Figure 18: History Tab for DBeaver Operator ID

Once you have made all the changes, click on the *"Save"* button to save the changes.

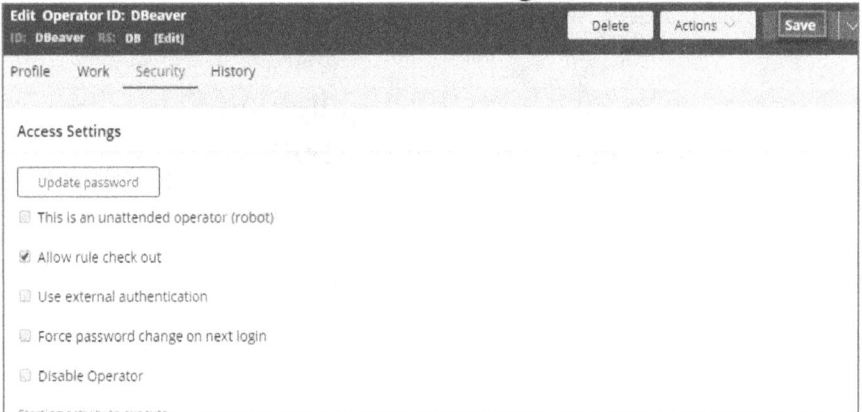

Figure 19: Saving Operator ID Changes

Testing the DBeaver User

First, logout from the current operator by clicking on the operator icon on the top right, followed by clicking on the "*Log off*", as shown below.

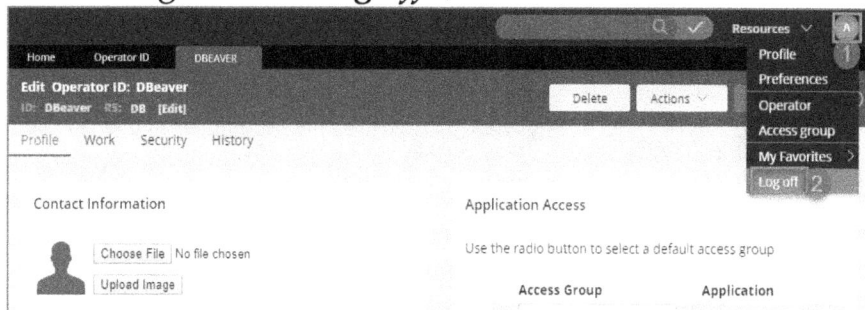

Figure 20: Logout from Pega

After logout, by default, you would be presented with the login screen. Enter the "*DBeaver*" username and its corresponding password [*rules*], followed by clicking on the "*Log in*" button.

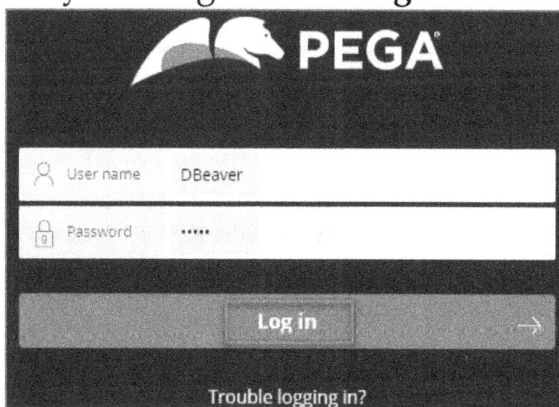

Figure 21: Login as DBeaver

The most important thing that you need to validate after login is that the *"Application"* shown should relate to your newly added application access group, as shown below.

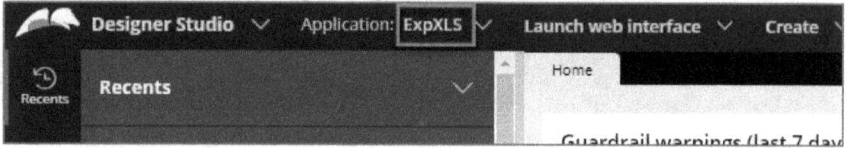

Figure 22: Sample Showing ExpXLS Selected as the Current Application

Note: *The above screenshot shows that of "ExpXLS" application, however, you should be looking for the "DBRest" instead.*

Yes, I know, I am nagging a lot here, but that is what I always do to my students, till the moment when they are able to jump in and say: "Stop! I know I should be looking for **DBRest***, not ExpXLS! "*

Note: *If the given user has multiple application access groups, you would need to click on the current application, followed by navigating to "Switch Application" and then clicking on your desired application to switch to.*

Granting Existing User with Access to The New Application

In this section, we will look at how to grant existing user, with access to our new application.

Note: *The following example is assuming that you are granting the access to " DBeaver". If you are granting the access for other user, use that user's name for the following instruction instead.*

In the top right corner of Designer Studio, do the following:

1) Enter *"DBeaver"* in the search box
2) Click on the search button

Figure 23: Searching for DBeaver Operator ID

In the search result below, click on the *"DBeaver"*.

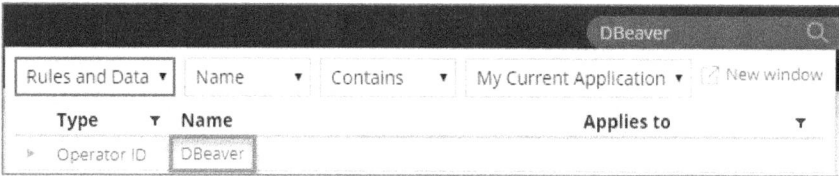

Figure 24: Search Results for Operator ID

With the Operator ID rule opened, perform the following:

1) Click on the "+" icon to add a new Access Group
2) In the new row of Access Group, enter the access group as: *DBRest:Administrators*
3) Click the Radio button beside this new access group to set it as the default
4) Click the "Save" button to save the profile

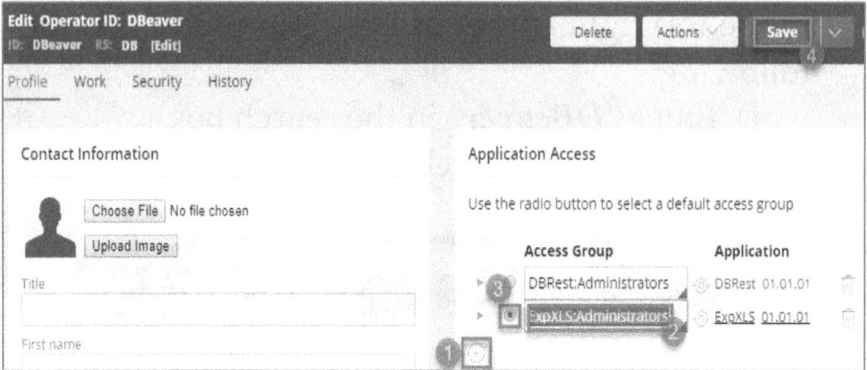

Figure 25: Example of Adding "ExpXLS:Administrators" Access Group to Existing Operator

Once saved, logout from the current user and then login as *DBeaver*.

Once login, apart from the default application, you should also see a list of other applications that *DBeaver* can switch to, as shown below.

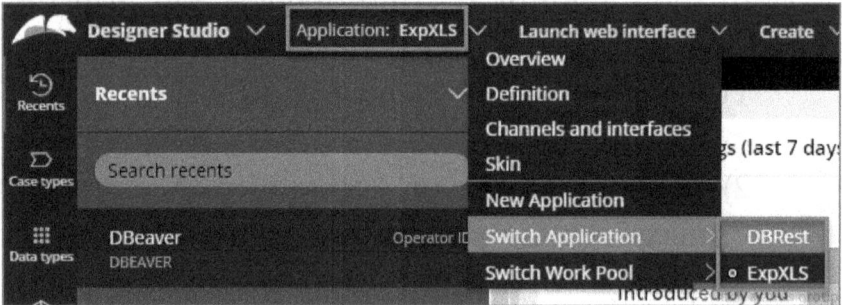

Figure 26: Example of DBeaver With 2 Application Access Groups

With the application and test user created, we can proceed to the next step.

Part 2: Creating the REST Service and REST Connector

Introduction to REST Service

In its simplest form, there are only 3 things to create in order to implement a Pega REST Service, they are:
1) REST Package
2) Service REST
3) Service REST Activity

REST Package

REST Package basically provides you with a container for the REST service itself.

In its simplest form, a REST package defines the IP address, and the base URL of the Service REST.

Service REST

Service REST provides the implementation of the various methods that you want to provide, such as GET, POST, PUT and DELETE.

💡 *Note: In Pega V8.x, there is a new PATCH method!*

Service REST Activity

What each of the Service REST method performs is specified using Pega Activity.

As you can see, it is as simple as that!

💡 *Note: Of course, we can always complicate things, but let's stay focus on getting the REST service up and running first!*

Creating the REST Package

In "*Records Explorer*": Under the "*Integration-Resources > Service Package*", right-click on it and select "*Create*".

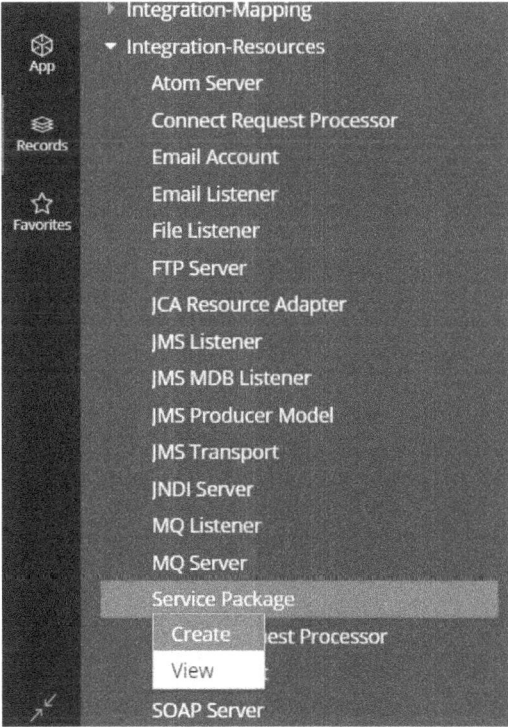

Figure 27: Creating a REST Package

In the opened form, enter the following (or whatever description you like), then click the *"Create and open"*.

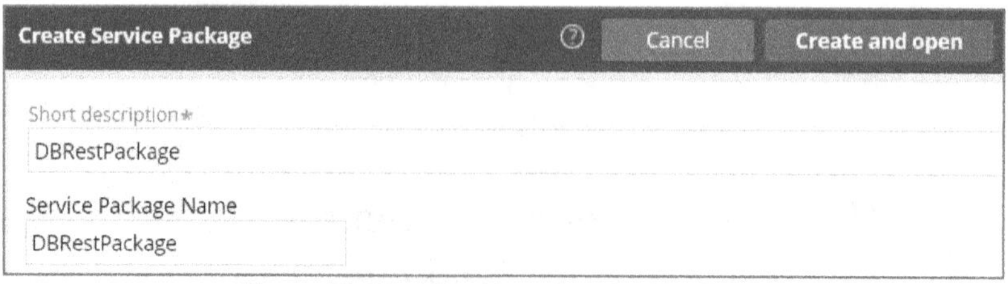

Figure 28: Naming Your Service Package

In the following rule, select a Service access group, in this case, *"DBRest:Administrators"*, followed by unticking the *"Requires authentication"*.

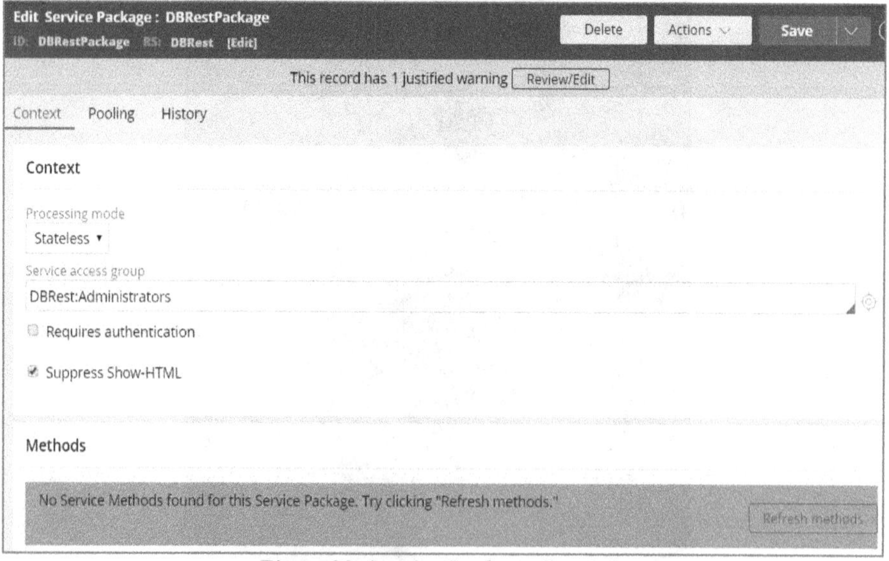

Figure 29: Service Package Created

Well, the Service package creation is done, simple!

Note: *It is better to have a standalone access group, such as* **"DBRest:DBRestAPI"***, and also to have the* **"Requires** **authentication"** *ticked. However, for demo and simplification purposes, we are skipping those for now.*

Creating the Service REST

G oing to the *"Records Explorer"*, under the *"Integration-Services > Service REST"*, right-click on it and select "**Create**".

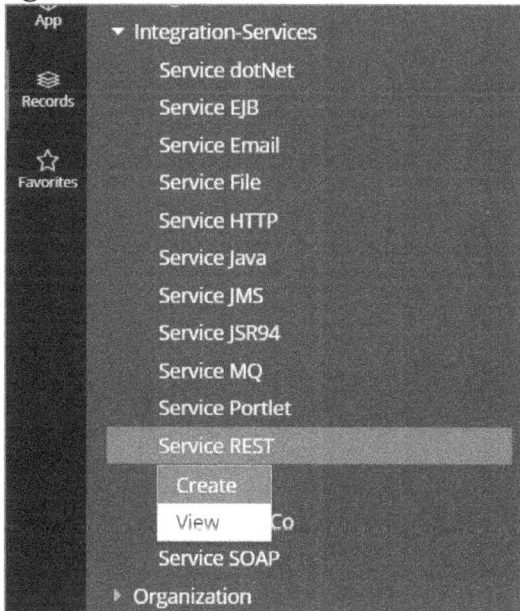

Figure 30: Creating a Service REST

In the opened form as shown below, there are basically 4 inputs, enter those accordingly.

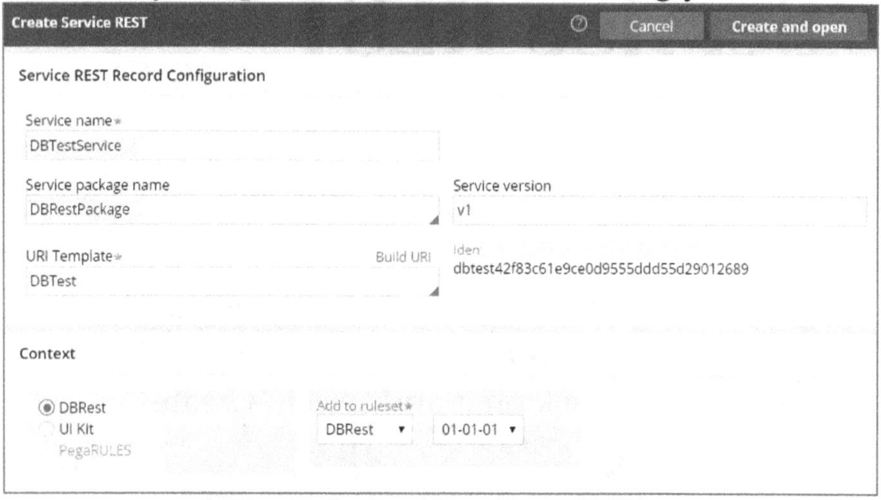

Figure 31: Configuration of Service REST

Rather than trying to explain what each of the above represents, it is easier to explain by showing you how those are being used by Pega.

After you have clicked the *"Create and open"* button, the following will be shown:

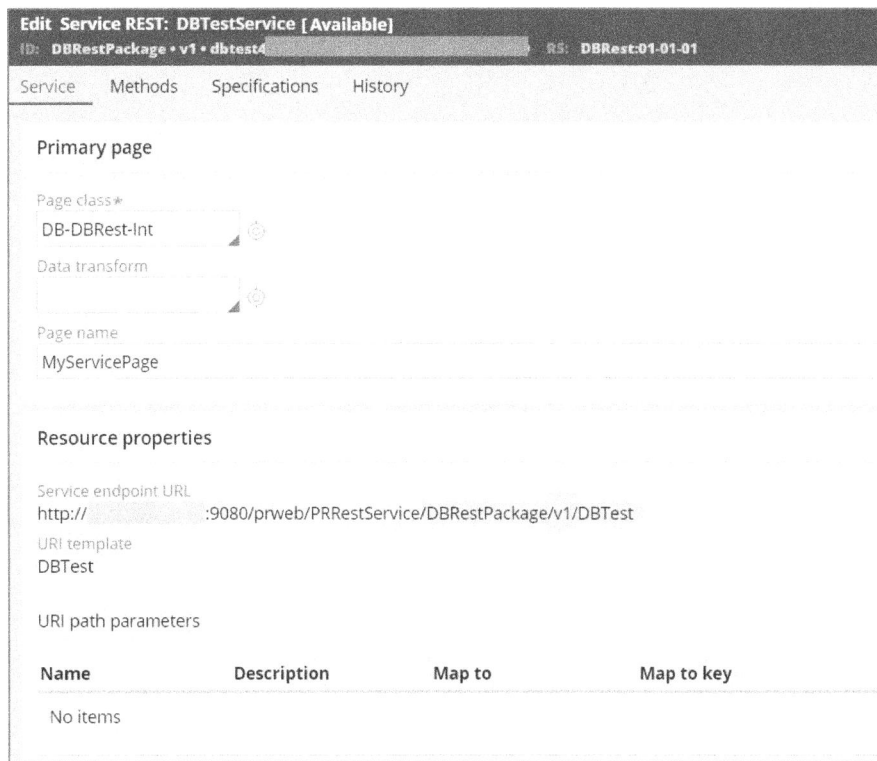

Figure 32: Service REST – DBTestService

As you observed:

- *Service name:* This is the name that you give to the rule
- *Service package name:* This allows you to group related Service REST into the same package, such that they will have the same IP address and base URL
- *Service version:* Allows you to specify version for the same Service REST

- **URI Template:** Enables you to specify additional string to add to the base. This usage enables users to pass parameters through the URL, instead of using the Query String

> **Note:** In the above diagram, you will notice that the "**Page class***" has a value of "**DB-DBRest-Int**". You need to provide a value for this before you can save this rule.

> **Note:** For the "**Page class***", generally, you should specify some relevant class for your specific situation. However, in my case, I had specified it as "**DB-DBRest-Int**", where "DB" is the ORG NAME, **DBRest** is the application name. The implication is that all other related rules, such as the various activities for the methods would be stored under this class.

> **Note:** Class structure and inheritance is a big topic in Pega. If I were to bring it here, it would just cause a lot of confusion. Therefore, I had designed this How-to Guide such that there is practically no need for you to know about the class structure and inheritance. If you need to, you can always add that in and move the rules to the relevant location.

Oh, by the way, just in case you didn't realise, your Service REST is already working!

Notice the URL under the *"Service endpoint URL"*? If you copy that URL to the Chrome browser, you will be able to get the output. Of course, you will get nothing since you have not implemented anything yet. So let's do this now!

Implementing HelloWorld Service REST GET Method

In general, GET method is the simplest to implement and test. If you are not passing in any header info, you could simply use a Chrome browser to do that.

Click on the *"Methods"* tab of the Service REST rule. You will be presented with 4 methods to choose from (GET/POST/PUT/DELETE).

Expand the *"GET"* method, the configuration for *"GET"* method will be displayed.

It may look intimidating, but actually, there are only 3 things that you need to be concerned with:
- Activity name
- Request
- Response

Note: *In Pega V8.x, you have another PATCH method.*

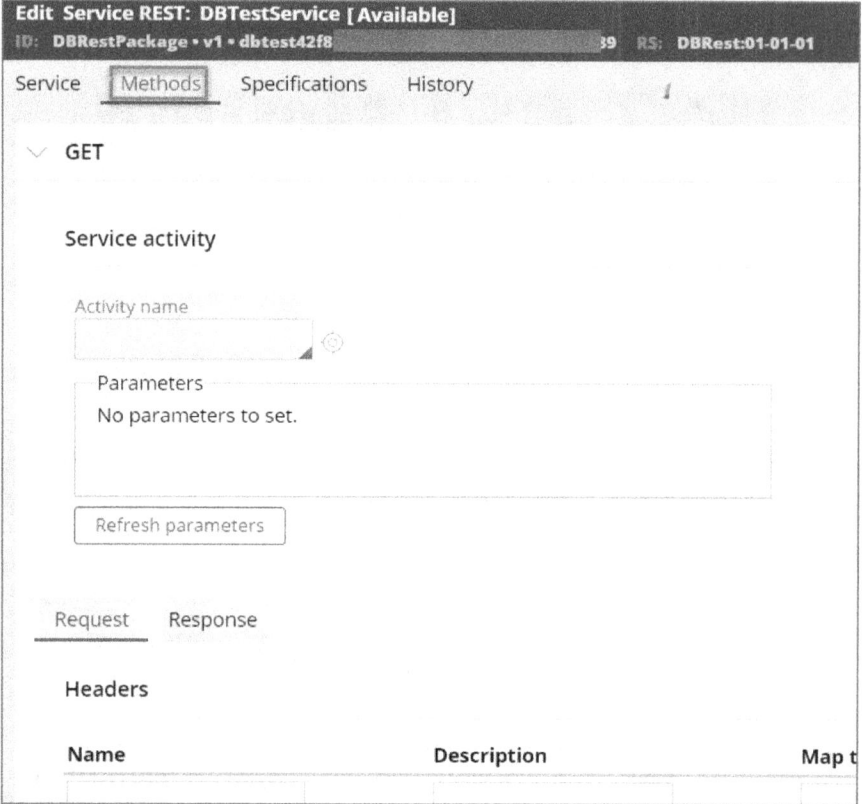

Figure 33: Service REST's GET Method

The *"activity name"* specifies the activity that you want to run when this Service REST's *"GET"* method is invoked.

The "*Request*" allows you to define the input that you pass in, while the "*Response*" specifies the output from the service.

Creating the Service Activity

Let's specify the activity name as "*DoDBTestGET*" and click on the icon on the right to create it.

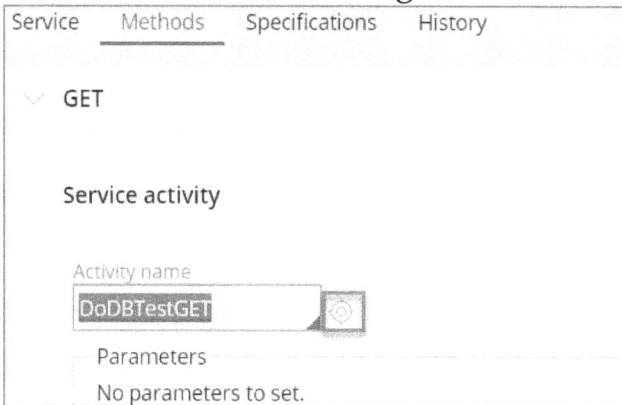

| Service | Methods | Specifications | History |

GET

Service activity

Activity name

DoDBTestGET

Parameters
No parameters to set.

Figure 34: Adding an Activity Name to GET Method

In the opened form that is shown below, take the default and click on the "*Create and open*" button.

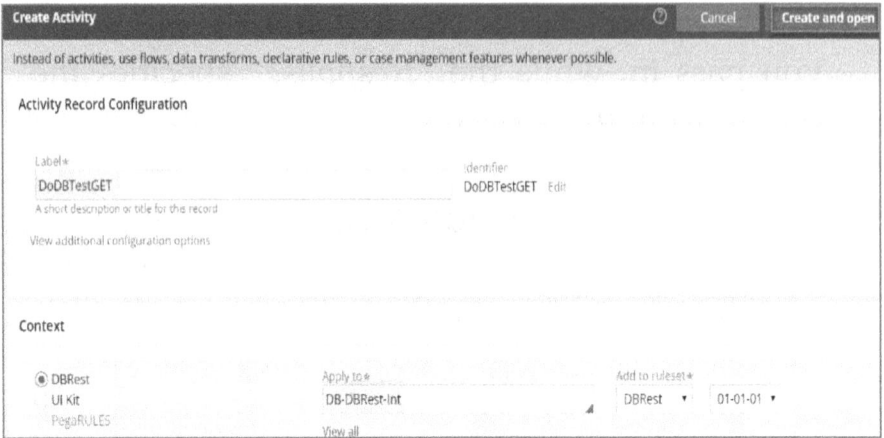

Figure 35: Naming the DoDBTestGET Activity

The following shows the created activity. Just click "*Save*". We will keep the activity empty for now.

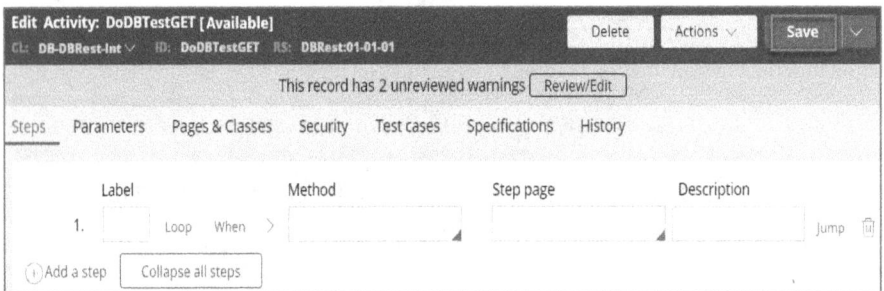

Figure 36: The Initial DoDBTestGET Activity

Specifying the Request and Response

For a start, let's not take in any parameters, so we shall keep the "*Request*" form empty, as follows:

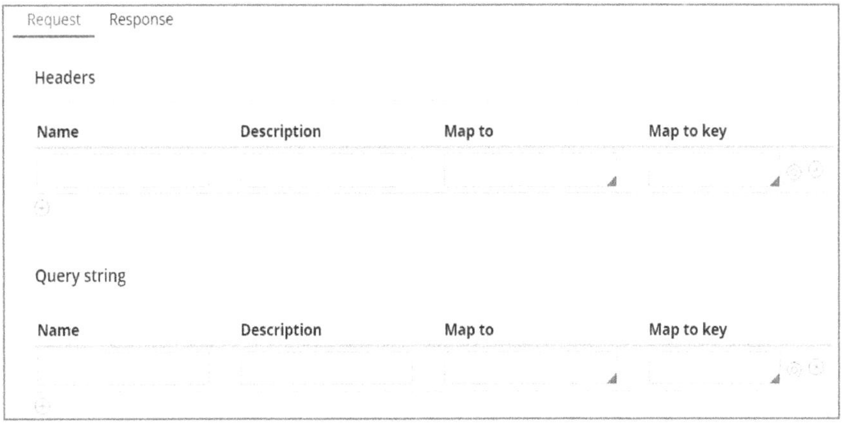

Figure 37: Default Empty Request Form for GET Method

For the "**Response**" form, there are basically 3 things that we need to set:

- Content Type
- Status Code
- Actual Response

"**Content Type**" tells the caller, such as the browser, what type of information we are passing back. In our case, we will be returning the data as "**JSON**".

"**Status Code**" specifies the outcome of the call. For example, if there is a server error, we will return "**500**", if it is a success, we will return "**200**".

> **Note:** Do you find the "**Status Code**" of "500" and "200" familiar? Yes, those are the standard HTTP error code!

As for the *"Actual Response"*, we can return some headers as well as the actual message data.

For a start, we will not return any headers, but focus only on the message data.

There are many ways to specify how you are going to return the data. You could return the data as a Clipboard, Constant, JSON, XML Stream, HTML Stream, etc.

However, we will use a method that would work for all cases and one that is very easy to implement and manage.

In this case, let's configure the *"Response"* tab as follows:

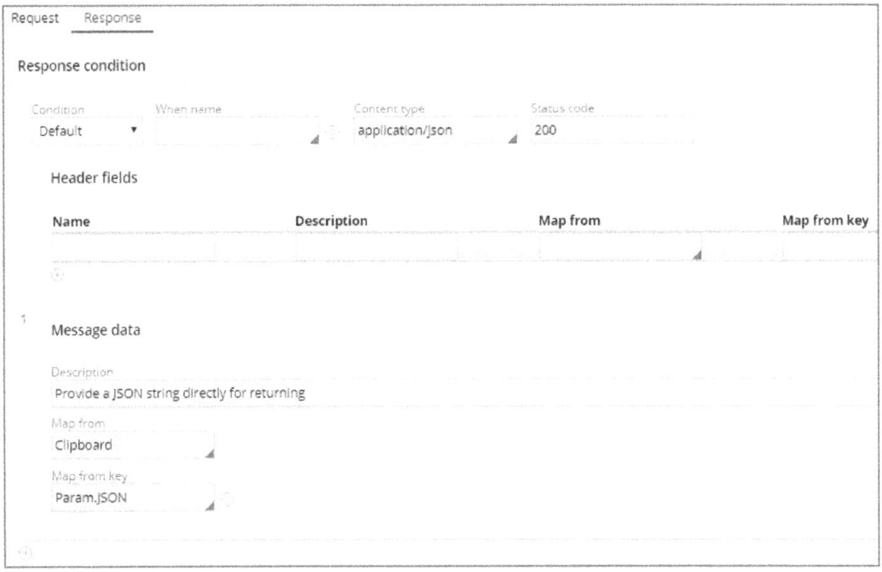

Request   Response

Response condition

Condition   When name   Content type   Status code
Default   ▼   application/json   200

Header fields

Name   Description   Map from   Map from key

Message data

Description
Provide a JSON string directly for returning

Map from
Clipboard

Map from key
Param.JSON

Figure 38: Configuration for Response of GET Method

From the above, we have configured the *"Content Type"* to be *"application/json"*, *"Status code"* as *"200"*.

Status code of *"200"* basically said that it is always a success, which we should not be doing blindly. However, since this is a quick illustration we shall proceed as such first.

For the message data, we are going to provide a properly formatted JSON string to be returned to the caller directly. This is generally the easiest and most manageable approach.

> 💡 *Note: Variables in Pega is denoted by "Param". So if you are declaring a variable called "JSON", it is represented as "Param.JSON".*
>
> *In this case, our service activity will prepare this "Param.JSON" for us.*

> 💡 *Note: Think of "Param" as some forms of global parameters, to be more precise, if you had done Servlet, etc, before, it is similar to those "Request variables", which has a 'page scope', something that could actually be lost if you do not propagate it down the chains of calls.*
>
> *In my other upcoming books, I will explain to you how to avoid the param altogether and use a different approach, which give you more control and traceability. It is something that is a bit 'naughty', but in a real-world implementation, it is more practical and reliable.*

Implementing the Service Activity for GET Method

So now, the job of the service activity is very simple. All we need to do is to make sure that it returns the variable *"Param.JSON"*, which is a JSON formatted string.

We could try to manually formulate the JSON string, but that would be too tedious! An easier way is to leverage on the Pega structure, and then convert it automatically to a JSON string.

Back to the *"DoDBTestGET"* that we created earlier, perform the following.

Pages & Classes Tab

In the *"Pages & Classes"* tab, enter the *"Page name"* as *"MyResponse"* and the *"Class"* as *"$ANY"*, as shown below:

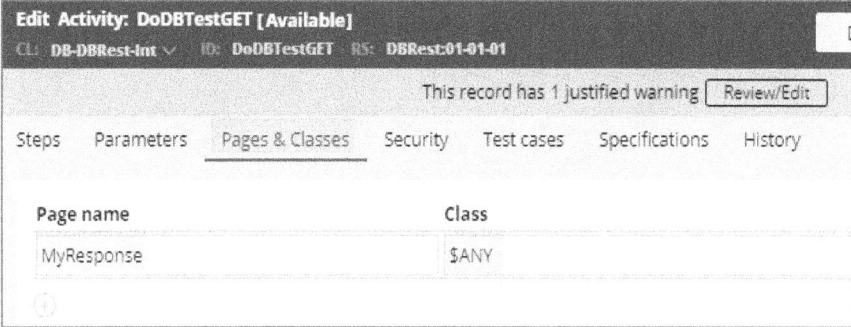

Edit Activity: DoDBTestGET [Available]

CL: DB-DBRest-Int ⌄   ID: DoDBTestGET   RS: DBRest:01-01-01

This record has 1 justified warning [Review/Edit]

Steps   Parameters   Pages & Classes   Security   Test cases   Specifications   History

Page name	Class
MyResponse	$ANY

Figure 39: Pages & Classes Tab for a Minimalistic REST GET Method

> **Note:** *The class type of "$ANY" basically tells Pega not to be bothered to validate the structure and allow me to do it any way I want it. Generally, it is not recommended, but for a demo and quick test, it is much easier for you to take this approach than to be bothered with all the classes and properties creation!*
>
> *In later chapters, I will explain why in some situations, it does not make any practical sense to define all the properties right up front!*

> **Note:** *You may have noticed that the class type of "$ANY" is used extensively by Pega, of course if you understand the purpose and implementation, like I do, you are free to use it! However, make sure you are able to justify the advantages of using it versus not! BTW, nobody will ask you in CLSA exams, you are not supposed to be talking about this in the first place!*

Steps Tab

In the *"Steps"* tab, enter the following:

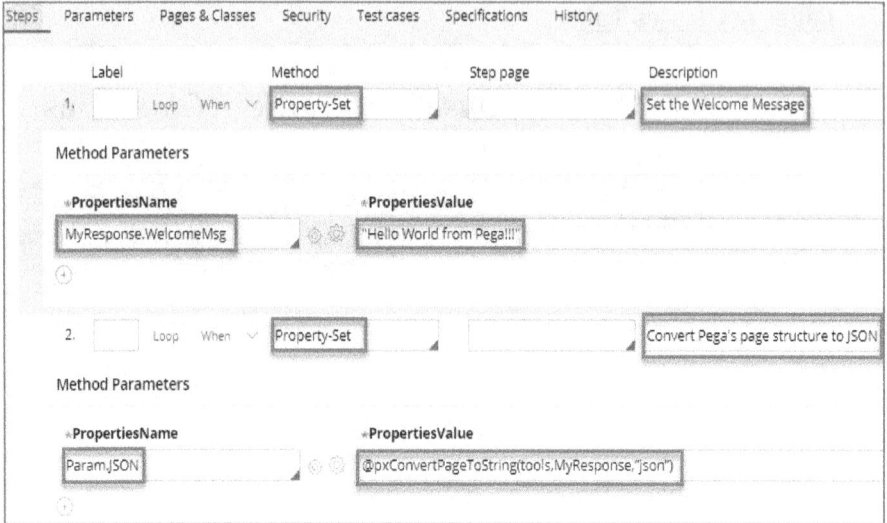

Figure 40: Configuring GET Service Activity to Return Pega Hello World!

Basically, there are only 2 steps:
1) Set the "Hello World from Pega!!!" string

MyResponse.WelcomeMsg	"Hello World from Pega!!!"

2) Convert that string into JSON

Param.JSON	@pxConvertPageToString(tools, MyResponse, "json")

> **Note:** The function **"pxConvertPageToString"** is OOTB. There is also a corresponding function **"pxConvertStringToPage"**! So, with these 2 functions, we are free to convert from JSON to Pega structure for manipulation and from Pega structure to JSON for returning!

> **Note:** Generally, it is a good practice to remove all unused pages, in this case the **"MyResponse"** page. This is usually done at the last step of the activity, using the **"Page-Remove"** method.

Testing the REST GET Method

Yes, you are right, we are now ready to test it! Now, go back to your *"Service REST"* and copy the *"Service endpoint URL"*. The following screen shows you the location of the URL:

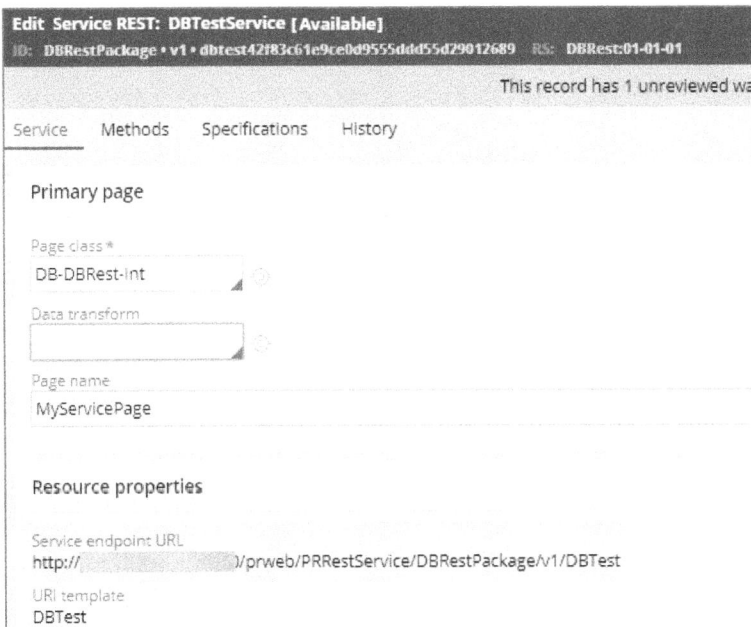

Figure 41: Getting the Service REST URL for Testing

Copy that URL and paste it into your browser! You should be able to get the following output:

Figure 42: Testing Pega REST Service Using GET Method Through Browser

> **Note:** *Invoking REST GET method works in Chrome and Firefox, but not in Internet Explorer and Microsoft Edge browsers!*

Implementing HelloWorld Service REST POST Method

Now, let's turn our attention to the POST method. Actually, the POST method structure is very similar to that of the GET method.

The 3 things that need to be implemented are still the same:
- Activity name
- Request
- Response

However, POST method allows you to send a JSON formatted string as input, while the GET method doesn't!

Creating the Service Activity

Similarly, let's create the activity for the POST method, giving it the name of *"DoDBTestPOST"*, as shown below:

Figure 43: Specifying POST Method Service Activity

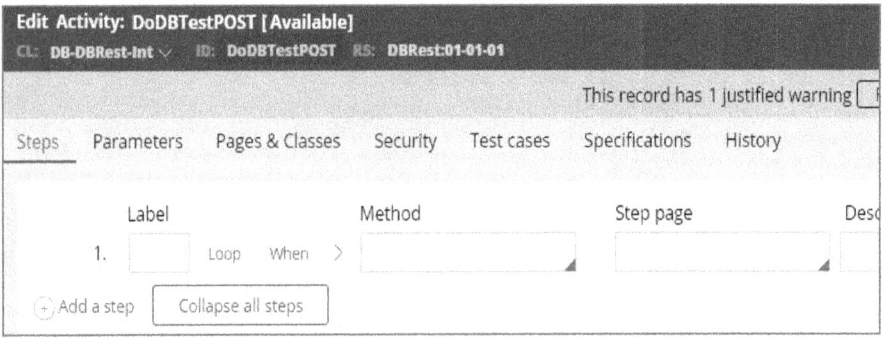

Figure 44: Service Activity for POST Method

As before, let's fill in the Request and Response first.

Specifying the Request and Response

Since the POST accept a JSON message format for both Request and Response, let's specify them as such.

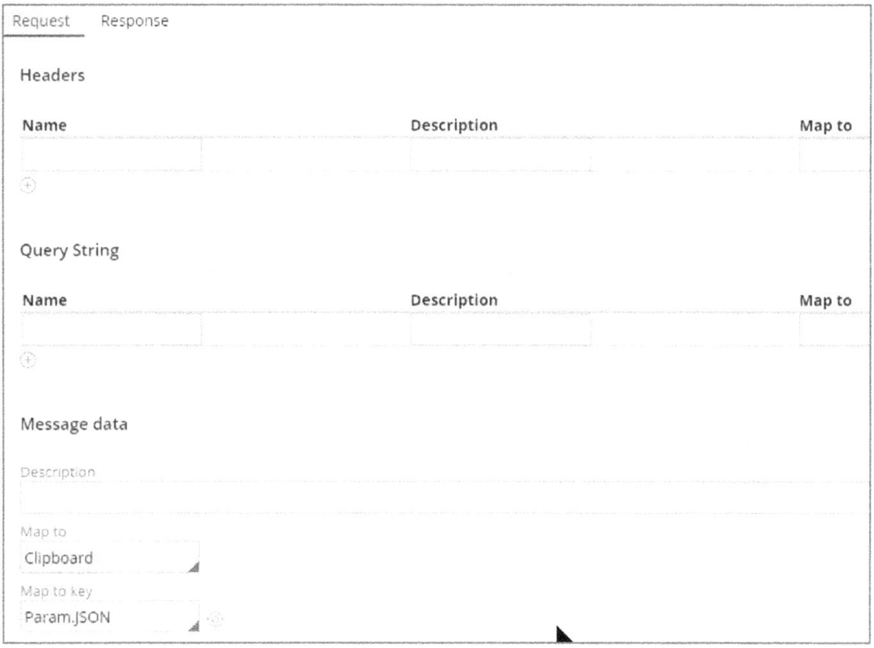

Request	Response

Headers

Name	Description	Map to

Query String

Name	Description	Map to

Message data

Description

Map to
Clipboard

Map to key
Param.JSON

Figure 45: REST Request "Message Data" for POST Method

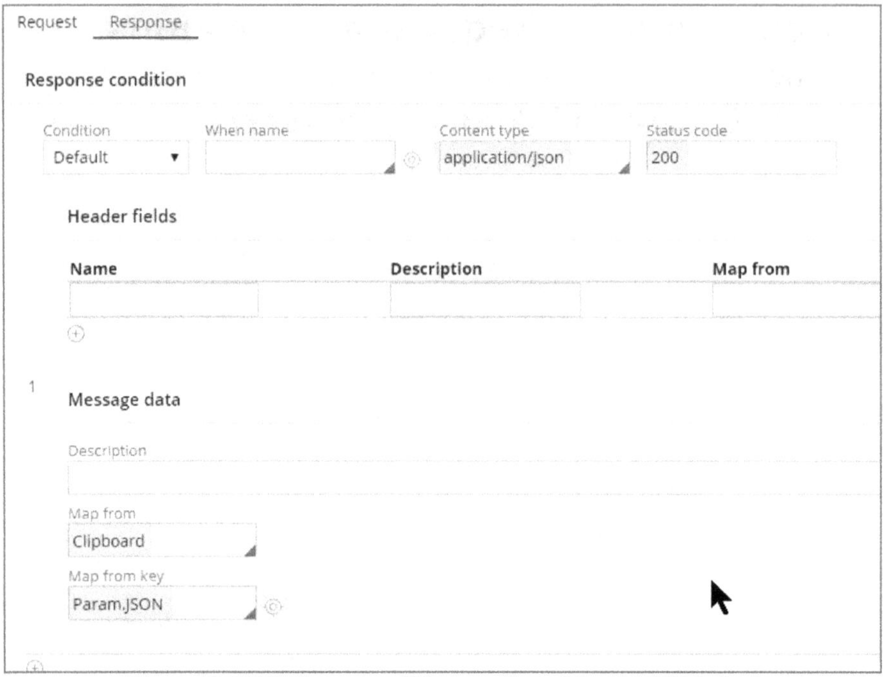

Figure 46: REST Response "Message Data" for POST Method

As you can see, it is relatively simple isn't it? Well, this is because I had simplified everything! I had moved away from the laborious class structure definition and different type of message data mapping and streamlined it into a single type, using *"Param.JSON"*. This approach could handle all possible scenario.

Implementing the Service Activity for POST Method

Similar to the GET method earlier, we now have Pega passing us the JSON input via the *"Param.JSON"*, as well as accepting the return through the same *"Param.JSON"*.

So, let's extend the earlier HelloWorld example. In this case, we will pass in our name for Pega to customize the *"HelloWorld"* message.

The following is the input JSON that we are supplying to the REST POST method:

```
{
    "name": "Debunkum Beaver"
}
```

Figure 47: Sample JSON Input for REST POST Method

Basically, there is only 1 parameter, which is the *"name"*, that we would be passing to Pega. Pega would then provide us with the personalised welcome message.

This time round, let's do it slightly differently. Remember that earlier for the GET method, in the *"Pages & Classes"* tab, we have defined the *"MyResponse"* as a page of type *"$ANY"*?

By doing that we had actually declared a clipboard page, named *"MyResponse"*.

If we were to use the same approach, we would need to define another *"MyRequest"* similar to the *"MyResponse"*.

Well, there is nothing wrong with that, but the clipboard page might start to get untidy.

> Note: *You can simply think of "Clipboard page" as some "Global Variables". To be more precise, it has only thread scope.*

Therefore, for this POST method, let's declare the *"MyRequest"* and *"MyResponse"* as a '*member variable*' of the *"DB-DBRest-Int"* class instead. At the same time, let's continue to specify its type to be *"$ANY"*.

Create MyRequest & MyResponse Page Properties
The following are the property settings for the *"MyRequest"* and *"MyResponse"* for the *"DB-DBRest-Int"* class:

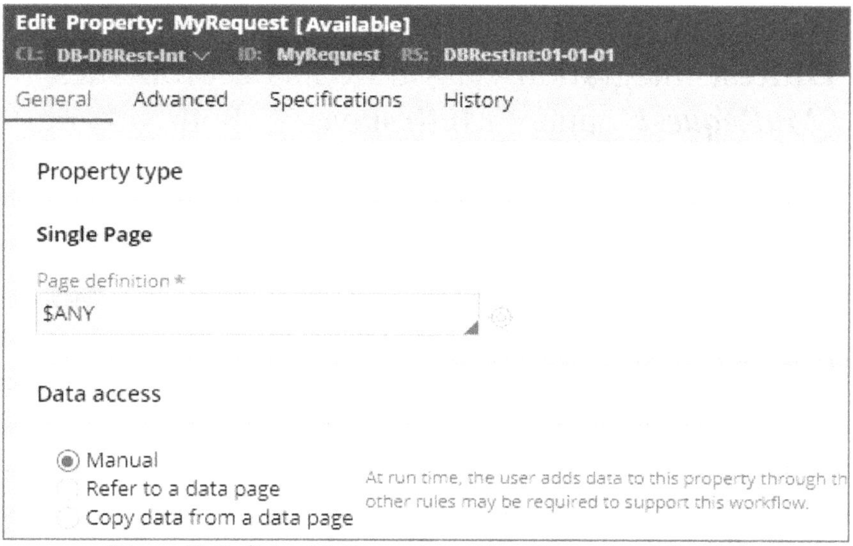

Edit Property: MyRequest [Available]
CL: DB-DBRest-Int ∨   ID: MyRequest   RS: DBRestInt:01-01-01

General   Advanced   Specifications   History

Property type

Single Page

Page definition *
$ANY

Data access

◉ Manual
　Refer to a data page   At run time, the user adds data to this property through th
　Copy data from a data page   other rules may be required to support this workflow.

Figure 48: Defining MyRequest as a Page Property of the DBRest Integration Class

Edit Property: MyResponse [Available]
CL: DB-DBRest-Int ∨   ID: MyResponse   RS: DBRestInt:01-01-01

General   Advanced   Specifications   History

Property type

Single Page

Page definition *
$ANY

Data access

◉ Manual
　Refer to a data page   At run time, the user adds data to this property through
　Copy data from a data page   other rules may be required to support this workflow.

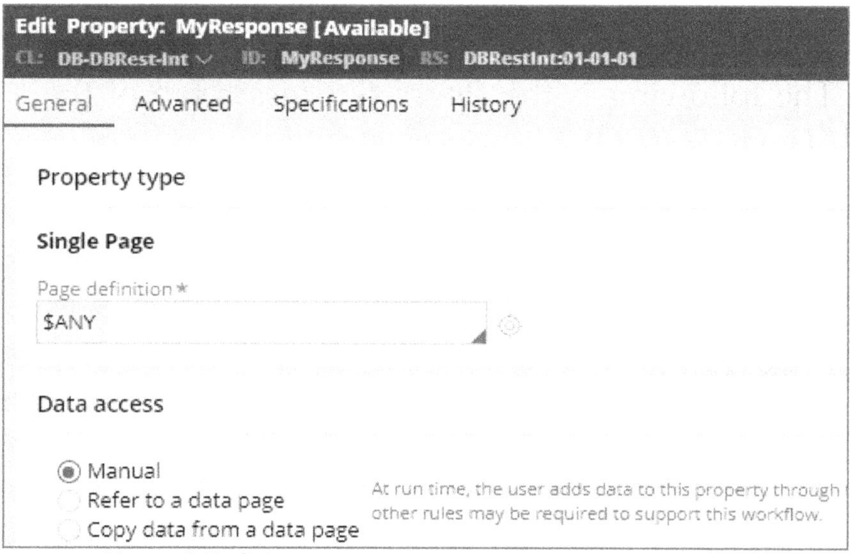

Figure 49: Defining MyResponse as a Page Property of the DBRest Integration Class

With the above declarations, basically, the **DBRest** integration class now has 2 properties: *"MyRequest"* and *"MyResponse"*, both are of Page type.

For the above 2 properties, *"MyRequest"* and *"MyResponse"*, we shall use that to store the <u>request message</u> passed to the class, and the <u>response message</u> that is produced by this integration class respectively.

Now let's update the *"DoDBTestPOST"* Service activity.

Pages & Classes Tab

The following is the *Pages & Classes* tab of the *"DoDBTestPOST"* service activity:

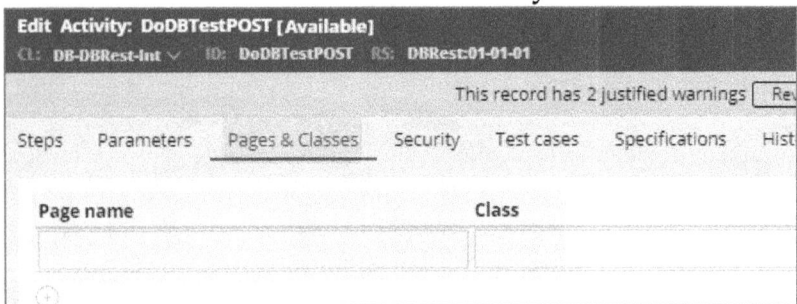

Figure 50: Pages & Classes Tab of DoDBTestPOST Service Activity

Since we had decided to use properties within the integration class itself, this tab is basically blank.

Steps Tab

The following are the steps for this service activity.

Step 1: Init values and convert the Param.JSON into MyRequest Page

1.	Loop	When	∨	Property-Set			Init values and convert the Param.JSON into MyRequest Page

Method Parameters

·PropertiesName			·PropertiesValue	
.MyRequest			""	
.MyResponse			""	
Param.MyStatus			@pxConvertStringToPage(tools..MyRequest, Param.JSON,"json")	

Figure 51: Step 1 of REST POST - Init values and convert the Param.JSON

In this step, we initialized both the "*.MyRequest*" and "*.MyResponse*", as well as making a call to the "*pxConvertStringToPage*" function to convert the "*Param.JSON*" into the "*.MyRequest*" page so that we can start manipulating it.

> **Note:** Recall in the "*Service REST: DBTestService*", I had told Pega to pass the Request message data as "*Param.JSON*"! That is why I am getting that "*Param.JSON*" and transforming it to the "*.MyRequest*" property of the Int class object, using the "*pxConvertStringToPage*" function.

Step 2: Handle error when the input is invalid

According to the specification of the function: "*pxConvertStringToPage*", if there is any problem, it will return false and set the error reason in "*Param.errorMessage*".

Therefore, in this step, we will create a *"When"* condition, that tests for *"Param.MyStatus==false"* as shown below:

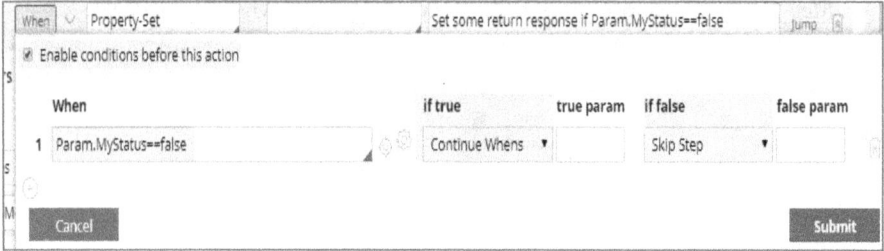

When	∨	Property-Set		Set some return response if Param.MyStatus==false		Jump	

☑ Enable conditions before this action

When	if true	true param	if false	false param
1 Param.MyStatus==false	Continue Whens ▾		Skip Step ▾	

Cancel   Submit

Figure 52: Step 2 of REST POST – When Rule

The step itself is as follows:

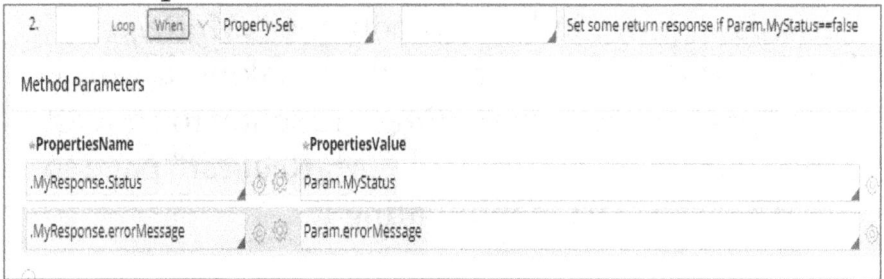

2.	Loop	When	∨	Property-Set		Set some return response if Param.MyStatus==false

Method Parameters

*PropertiesName	*PropertiesValue
.MyResponse.Status	Param.MyStatus
.MyResponse.errorMessage	Param.errorMessage

Figure 53: Step 2 of REST POST – Set Error Status and Message

Of course, this is not the best error handling, but just a quick demonstration to illustrate the idea.

> **Note:** Since error in the request message data would typically render all processing invalid, it is more appropriate to create some error code and return as a "500" error instead of the current hardcoded value of "200". In the Master Beaver Version, we will investigate that!

Step 3: Set the welcome message

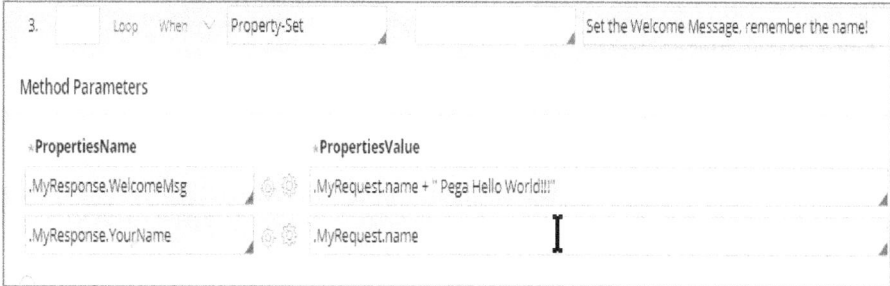

3.	Loop When ∨	Property-Set		Set the Welcome Message, remember the name!

Method Parameters

*PropertiesName	*PropertiesValue
.MyResponse.WelcomeMsg	.MyRequest.name + " Pega Hello World!!!"
.MyResponse.YourName	.MyRequest.name

Figure 54: Step 3 of REST POST - Set Welcome Message

In this step, we set the welcome message to be returned, as well as echoing the name that was passed in earlier.

Step 4: Convert Pega's page structure to JSON

In this last step, we convert the response message that we want to return, back into JSON format by using the function: *"pxConvertPageToString"*.

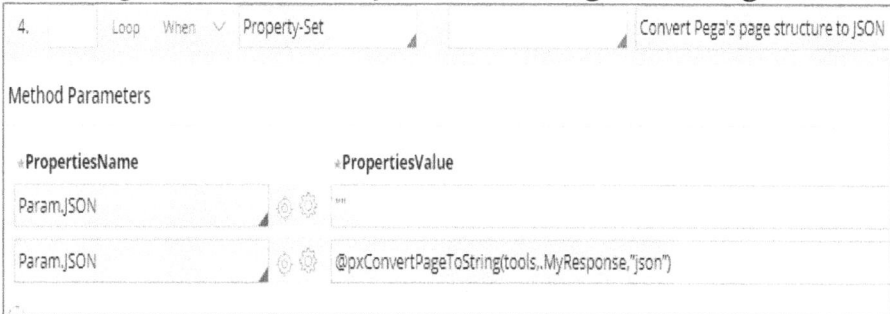

4.	Loop When ∨	Property-Set		Convert Pega's page structure to JSON

Method Parameters

*PropertiesName	*PropertiesValue
Param.JSON	""
Param.JSON	@pxConvertPageToString(tools,.MyResponse,"json")

Figure 55: Step 4 of REST POST - Convert Pega's Page Structure to JSON

Well, the implementation is completed, let's test it!

Testing the REST POST Method

To test the POST method, you cannot use the browser. You could use *SoapUI* or *Postman*. However, during development, it is still easier to use the **OOTB Pega testing tool**.

To access the **OOTB Pega testing tool**, perform the following.

Go back to your *"Service REST: DBTestService"*, click on the *"Actions"*, followed by the *"Run"*, as shown below:

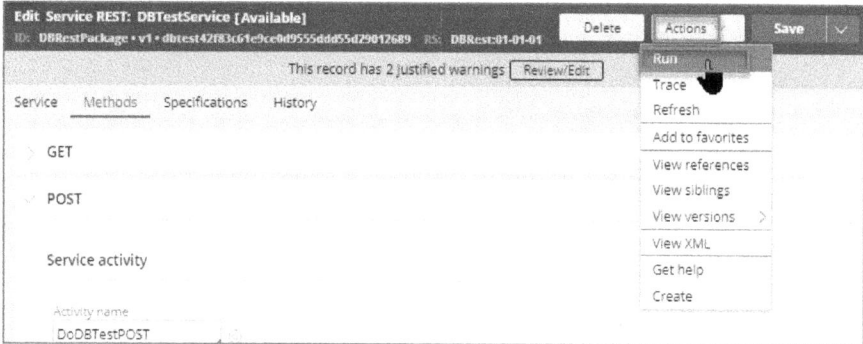

Figure 56: Launching Pega OOTB Service Testing Tool

In the dialog that opened, select *"HTTP Method"* as **"POST"**, providing the following sample JSON input:

```
{
  "name": "Debunkum Beaver"
}
```

The following is the sample screen. Click *"Execute"* to run it.

Requestor Context
- Use current requestor context
- Initialize service requestor context

Enter Request Data

Resource param Values
None

HTTP Method
- GET
- POST
- PUT
- DELETE

HTTP Header Values
None

Query String Values
None

Message Buffer
```
{
  "name": "Debunkum Beaver"
}
```

Execute

Figure 57: Running Pega OOTB Service Testing Tool

You will now get the following output:

Simulation Results for REST Service DBRestPackage.v1.dbtes

Overall Result

Success

List of Steps

STEP	RESULT
Lookup Service Properties	Not Attempted
Initialize Requestor	Not Attempted
Perform Authentication	Not Attempted
Initialize Primary Page	Success
Map Inbound Data	Success
Invoke Service Activity	Success
Determine Response Type	Success
Map Outbound Data	Success

Response Header Values

HEADER	VALUE
HTTP Status code	200

Response Parameter Values

DATA TYPE	VALUE
java.lang.String	{ "WelcomeMsg":"Debunkum Beaver Pega Hello World!!!" ,"YourName":"Debunkum Beaver" }

Figure 58: Sample Output from Pega OOTB Service Testing Tool

Well, that is cool, isn't it?

Implementing REST Connector

W e have successfully implemented REST Service in Pega. Now let's implement a *REST Connector* to invoke the service!

The normal way of creating a *REST connector* is to use the Wizard. To do that, navigate as follows: *Designer Studio > Integration > Connectors > Create REST Integration,* as shown below:

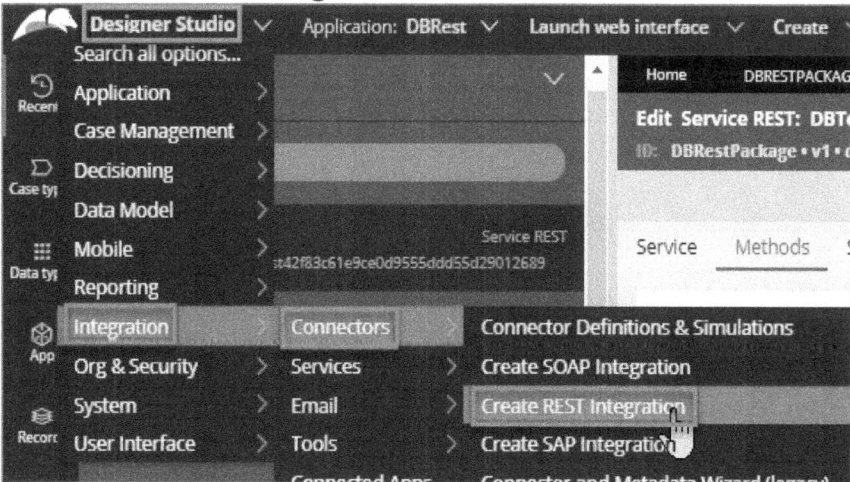

Figure 59: Launching the "Create REST Integration" Wizard

You will now be presented with the wizard as shown below:

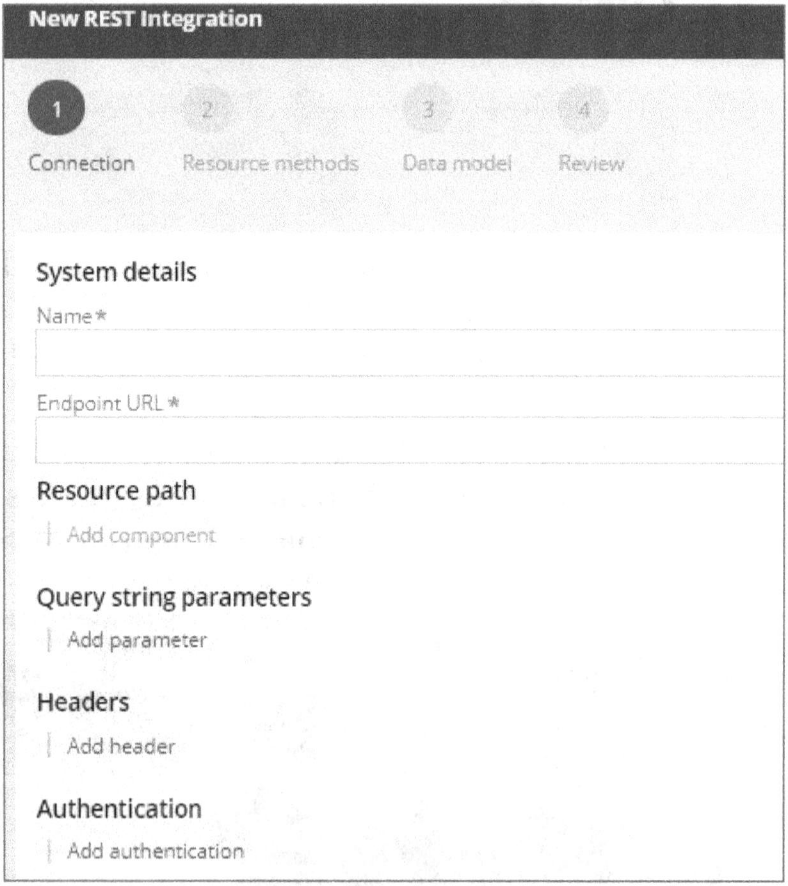

New REST Integration

① Connection   ② Resource methods   ③ Data model   ④ Review

System details

Name*

Endpoint URL*

Resource path

Add component

Query string parameters

Add parameter

Headers

Add header

Authentication

Add authentication

Figure 60: "Create REST Integration" Wizard

By following the 4 steps, you will be guided by the wizard to create the *REST Connector*. At the end of it, the wizard will automatically generate the required class structures of both the *request message* and *response message* for you.

Another useful capability is that you can test the invocation directly using the provided tool within the Wizard as shown below.

Using the Wizard Tool for Testing

In *Step 3* of the wizard, you can invoke the testing tool by clicking on the "*Add a REST response*" link, as shown below:

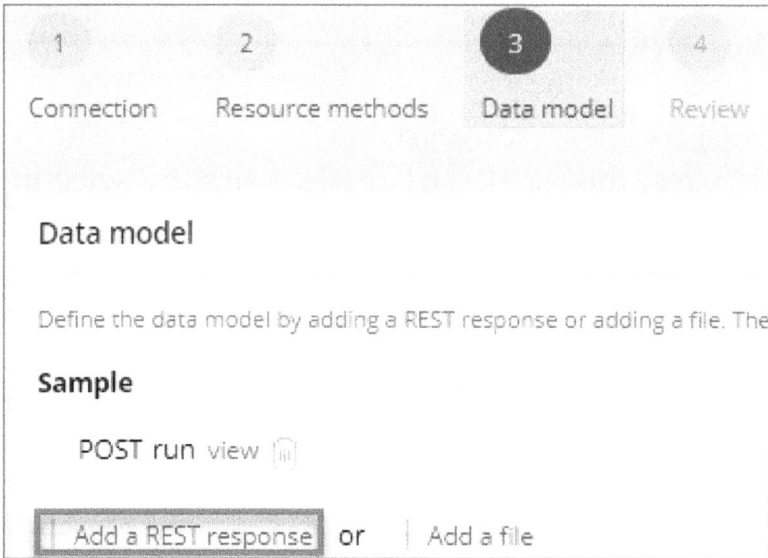

Figure 61: Add a REST Response to Invoke the Wizard Tool for Testing

In the opened dialog, you can choose the method to use.

> Note: The list of choices available in the "Choose method" dropdown
> list was selected in Step 2 (Resource methods)!

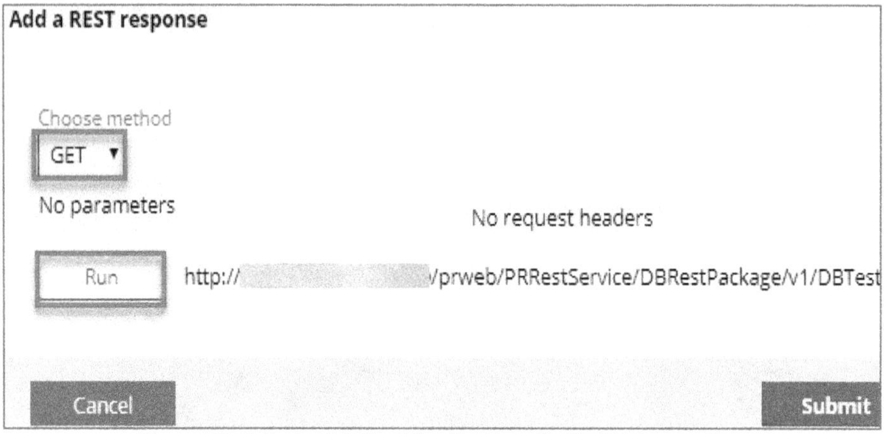

Add a REST response

Choose method

GET ▼

No parameters   No request headers

Run   http://   /prweb/PRRestService/DBRestPackage/v1/DBTest

Cancel   Submit

Figure 62: Select a Method for Testing the REST Invocation

Testing the REST GET Method

Let's test the REST GET method first by selecting the "*GET*" method, followed by clicking on the "*Run*" button.

The following shows the output:

Add a REST response

Choose method

GET ▼

No parameters   No request headers

Run   http://   /prweb/PRRestService/DBRestPackage/v1/DBTes

Response

Code: **200**   Body   Headers

```
1 {
2   "WelcomeMsg":"Hello World from Pega!!!"
3 }
4
```

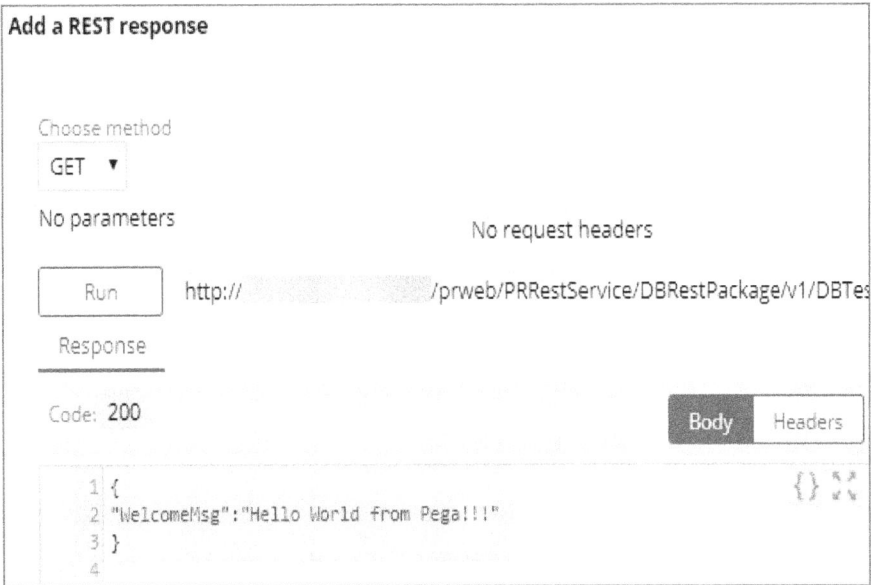

Figure 63: Testing the REST GET Method

Testing the REST POST Method

Now let's change the method to *"POST"*. Notice
that we are now provided with a *"Request text
area"* for us to enter the message data, with the
"Content type" initialised to *"JSON"* for us.

Add a REST response

Choose method

POST ▼

No parameters   No request headers

| Run | http://   /prweb/PRRestService/DBRestPackage/v1/DBTest

Request

Content type   JSON ▼

| 1 | {} ⋈

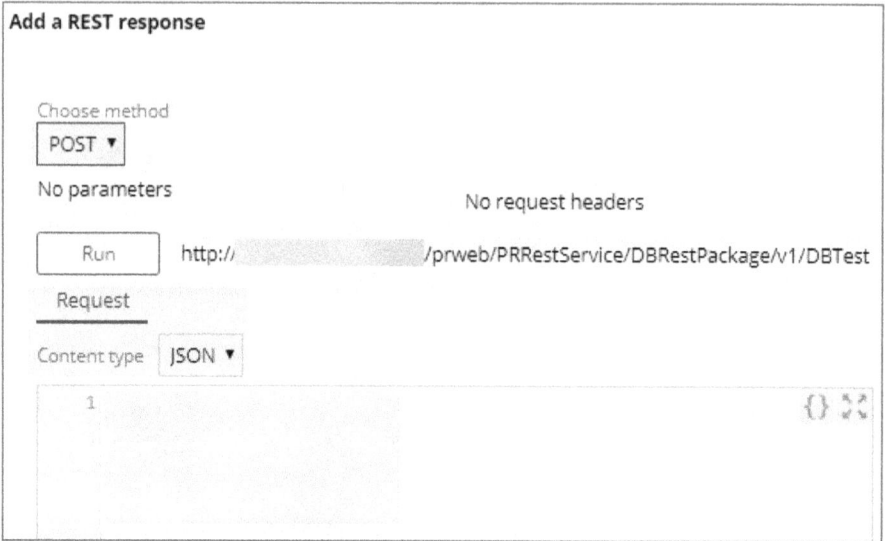

Figure 64: Sample REST POST Method Screen

Let's enter the earlier test JSON, followed by clicking the *"Run"* button.

```
{
    "name": "Debunkum Beaver"
}
```

As expected, we will get the *Response JSON* with the *"WelcomeMsg"* and the *"YourName"*, as shown below.

Add a REST response

Choose method

POST ▼

No parameters   No request headers

Run   http://_____/prweb/PRRestService/DBRestPackage/\

Request   Response

Code: 200   Body   He

```
1 {
2 "WelcomeMsg":"Debunkum Beaver Pega Hello World!!!"
3 ,"YourName":"Debunkum Beaver"
4 }
5
```

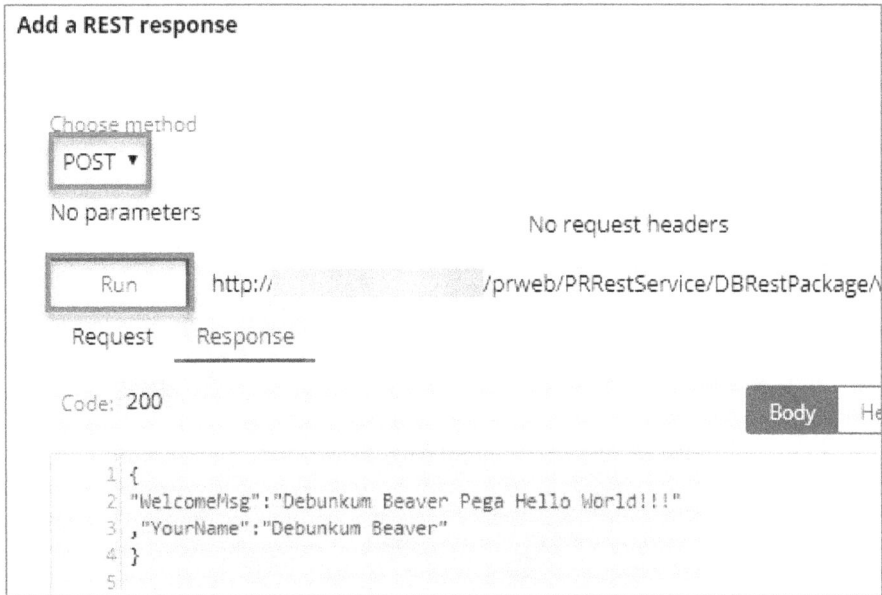

Figure 65: Testing the REST POST Method

Remember that we had done simple checks for invalid Request message data? So, let's test that too!

To do that, let's go back to the "*Request*" tab, and change the input to some <u>invalid JSON</u>, such as this, after that, click the "*Run*" button.

```
{
   "name": "Debunkum Beaver"
This is not JSON anymore...
}
```

As expected, we now have both the *"Status"* and *"errorMessage"* entries, with the *"Status"* having a value of *"false"* while *"errorMessage"* contains the actual reason for the failure.

```
Choose method
POST ▼
No parameters                              No request headers

  Run        http://_____/prweb/PRRestService/DBRestPackage/v1/DBTest

  Request    Response

Code: 200                                              Body    Headers

1 {
2 "errorMessage":"Exception occurred while adopting data onto the target page : I
  nvalid clipboard stream detected in module (unspecified).  Reason: (unspecifie
  d)"
3 ,"Status":"false"
4 ,"WelcomeMsg":" Pega Hello World!!!"
5 }
6
```

Figure 66: Testing the REST POST Method Using an Invalid JSON Input

> Note: The invalid JSON input should have return a code of 500 instead of 200, however, this is expected since we had hardcoded it as such! We will address this in the Master Beaver Edition.

Generally, using the *"REST Connector Wizard"* to create a REST Connector is very simple, intuitive, and useful.

However, there are 3 situations that would cause potential problems:

- Different REST responses for different scenario
- REST Service is in development and would be changed later
- Limitation of the length of the identifier

Different REST responses for different scenario

If the target REST Service returns different structure of responses for different outcome, it would not be feasible to provide all the possibilities or generate all the different outcome using the *"REST Connector Wizard"*.

REST Service is in development and would be changed later

If you are in parallel developments, or if the REST interface changed during development, going through the wizard again and again or manually adding / deleting those changed attributes would be horrendous!

Limitation of the length of the identifier

In Step 4 of the Wizard, the identifier for the generated rules is limited to 25 characters, as shown below.

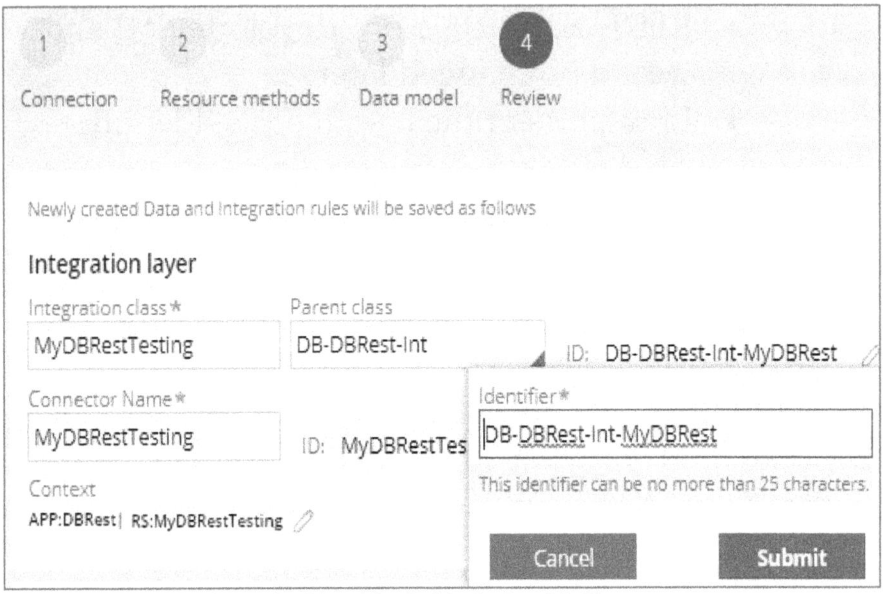

Figure 67: Identifier Is Limited to 25 Characters

You may not realise the implication of this problem now, but if you need to group various integrations into related classes, you will soon be forced to use very weird names!

Therefore, let's do it differently!

Manually Creating a REST Connector

Actually, it is easier to manually create the *REST Connector*. To do that, in the *"Records Explorer"*, just navigate as follows:

- Expand the *"Integration-Connectors"*
- Right-click on *"Connect REST"*
- Left-click on the *"Create"*

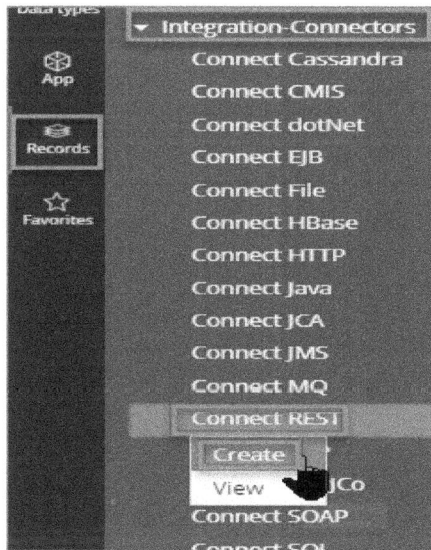

Figure 68: Connect REST Menu Navigation

In the form that opened, enter the following info, followed by clicking on *"Create and open"*.

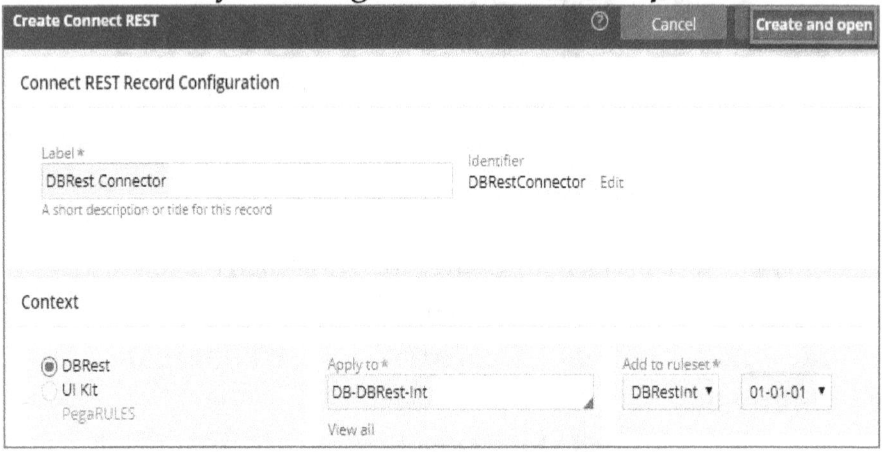

Figure 69: Connect REST Record Configuration

In the created rule, for the following tabs, enter the information accordingly.

Service Tab

Fill in the *"Resource path"* as the *"Service endpoint URL"* of the *Service REST*.

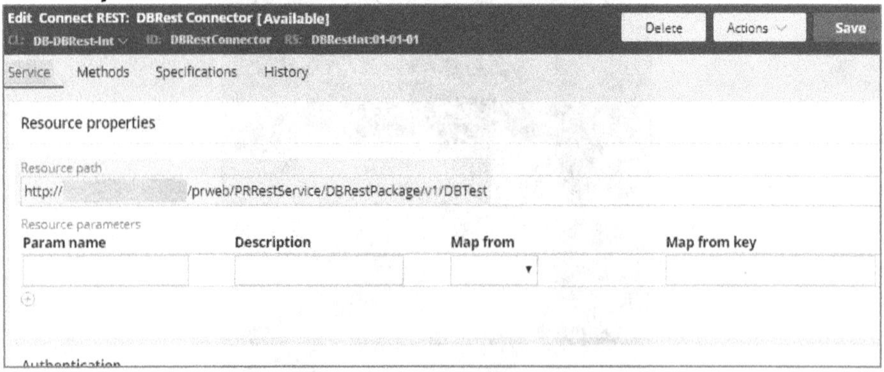

Figure 70: Service Tab of Connect REST

*Note: You can copy the "**Service endpoint URL**" from the earlier **Service REST**.*

Methods Tab

GET Method

In the ***Methods tab,*** for *"**Get**"*, under the *"**Response**"*, for the *"**Message Data**"*, specify it as follows:

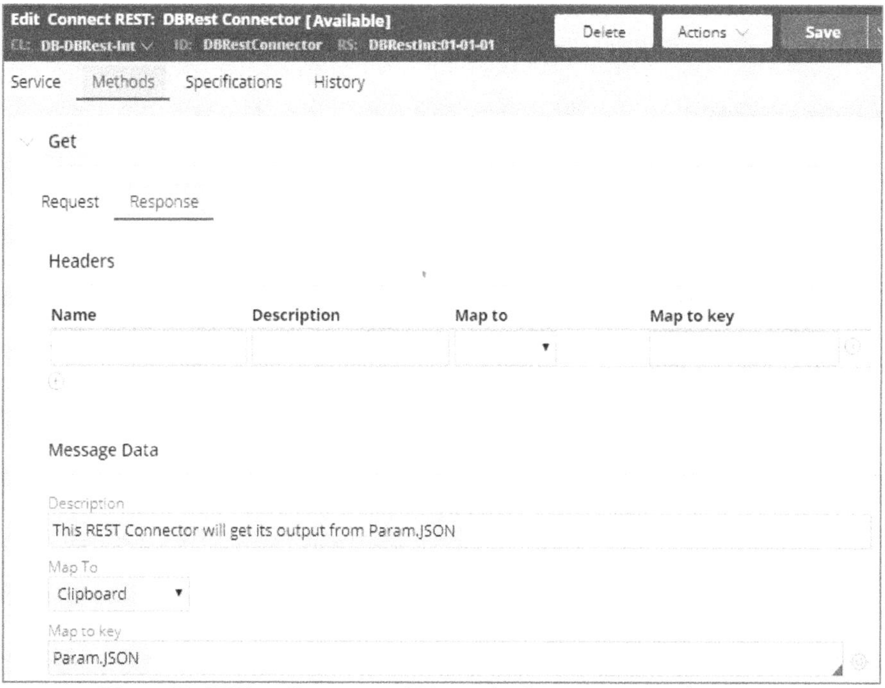

Figure 71: DBRestConnector GET Method Response Configuration

*Note: There is nothing to configure for the "**Request**" since this particular service of ours does not have any inputs!*

POST Method

Similarly, for the "*Post*", configure the "*Request*" and "*Response*" as follows:

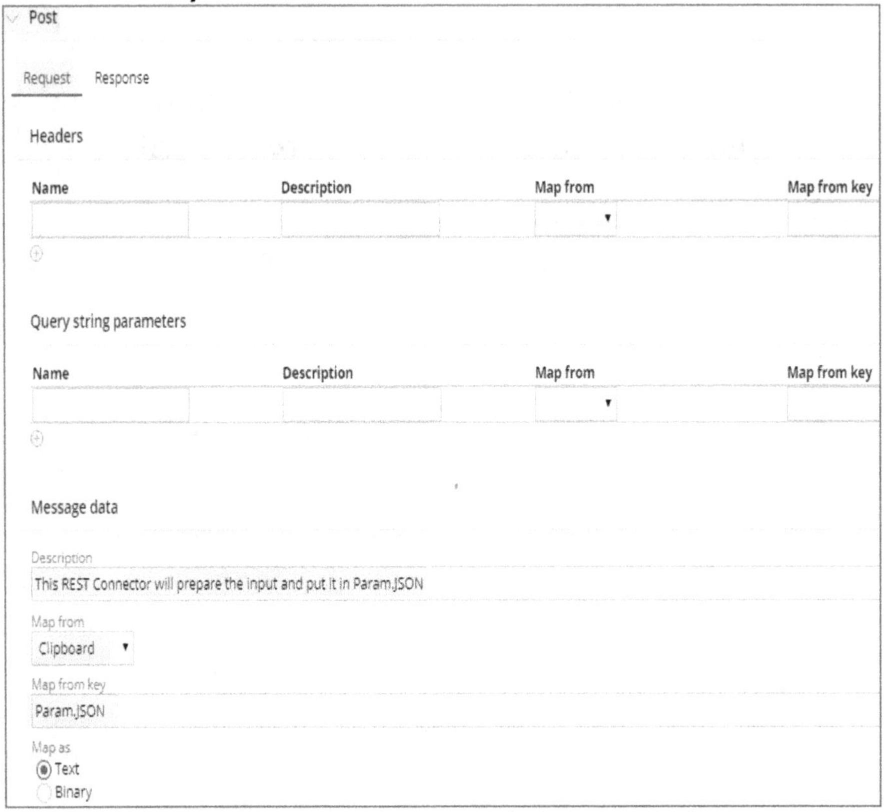

Post

Request   Response

Headers

Name	Description	Map from	Map from key
		▼	

⊕

Query string parameters

Name	Description	Map from	Map from key
		▼	

⊕

Message data

Description
This REST Connector will prepare the input and put it in Param.JSON

Map from
Clipboard   ▼

Map from key
Param.JSON

Map as
◉ Text
◯ Binary

Figure 72: DBRestConnector POST Method Request Configuration

Figure 73: DBRestConnector POST Method Response Configuration

OK! Our REST Connector is ready! It is now able to support both "GET" and "POST" method. The next step is to test our REST Connector.

To test the REST Connector, let's use a Datapage to do that!

Invoking a REST Connector Using Datapage

Technically, we could also use activity to invoke the REST service for testing. However, it is easier and better to use Datapage. Datapage provides options for you to cache the data, it also makes it much easier for testers and new users of Pega to use.

Datapage Configuration

The following shows the created datapage:

Edit Data Page: D_DBRestConnectorPOST [Available]
ID: D_DBRestConnectorPOST RS: DBRestInt:01-01-01

This recor

| Definition | Load Management | Parameters | Pages & Classes | Test cases | Usag |

Data page definition

Structure

| Page | ▼ |

Object type *

| DB-DBRest-Int | |

Edit mode

| Read-Only | ▼ |

Scope

| Thread | ▼ |

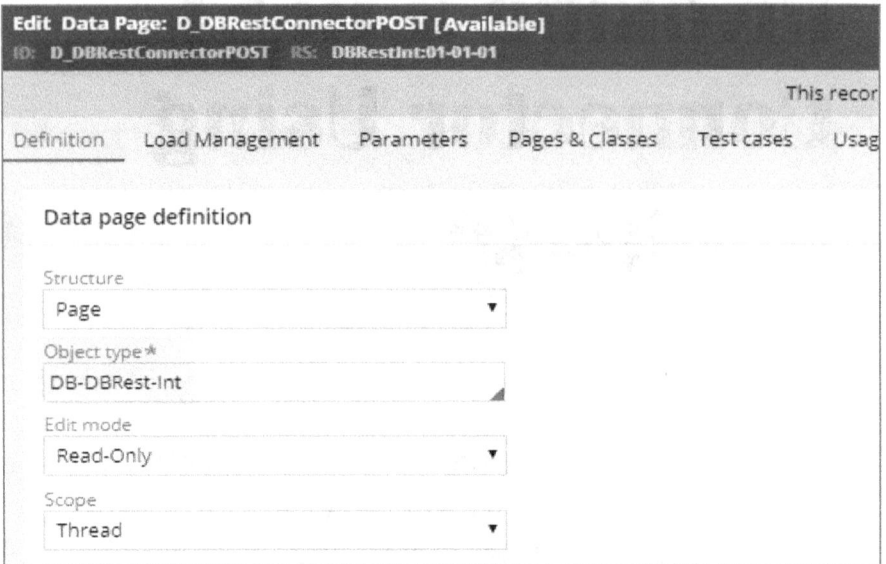

Figure 74: Datapage Used For Testing REST Service

Since the REST service that we created earlier is taking in a *"name"* parameter, let's configure this datapage to take in the *"name"* parameter too.

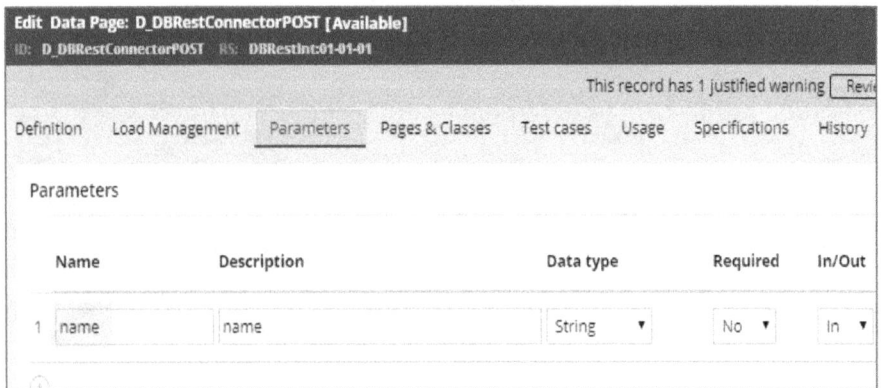

Edit Data Page: D_DBRestConnectorPOST [Available]
ID: D_DBRestConnectorPOST RS: DBRestInt:01-01-01

This record has 1 justified warning [Revi

| Definition | Load Management | Parameters | Pages & Classes | Test cases | Usage | Specifications | History |

Parameters

	Name	Description	Data type	Required	In/Out
1	name	name	String ▼	No ▼	In ▼

Figure 75: Parameters Tab of the Datapage Used for Testing REST Service

Under the *"Definition"* tab, scroll down to configure the *"Data sources"* as follows:

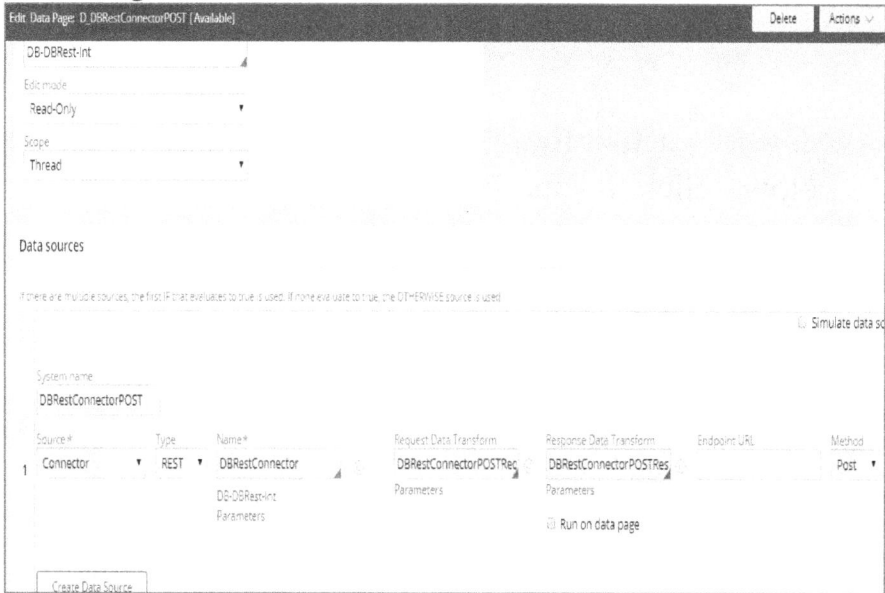

Figure 76: Configured the Data Sources as a REST Connector

In the above, we had selected as follows:

- *Source: Connector*
- *Type: REST*
- *Name: DBRestConnector (which is the REST connector that we created earlier.)*
- *Request Data Transform: DBRestConnectorPOSTRequest*
- *Response Data Transform: DBRestConnectorPOSTResponse*
- *Method: Post*

Also, for each of the *"Parameters"* links, as shown below, click it one-by-one and tick the *"Pass current parameter page"*.

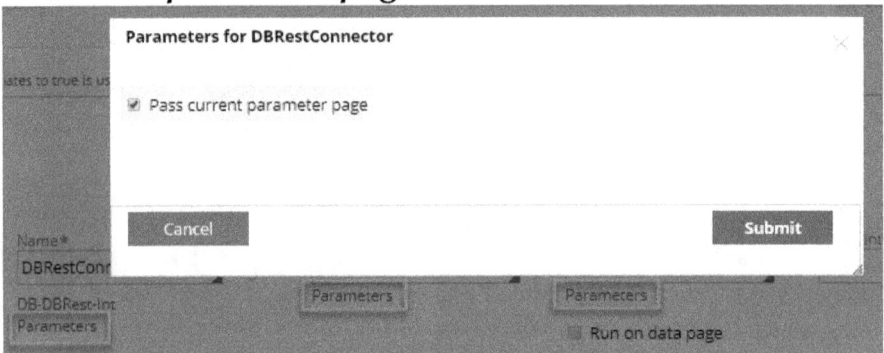

Figure 77: Propagating the Parameters to the Downstream Rules

Request Mapping Configuration

With the *"Request Data Transform"* field entered as: *"DBRestConnectorPOSTRequest"*, click on the icon on its right.

Creating REST Service and REST Connector

This will create the given rule for you. In this *"DBRestConnectorPOSTRequest"* mapping rule, we need to set the request that we would be passing over to the REST service via the *"Param.JSON"* parameter, using the JSON format.

Parameters Tab

Firstly, in the *"Parameter"* tab, define the *"name"* parameter as follows:

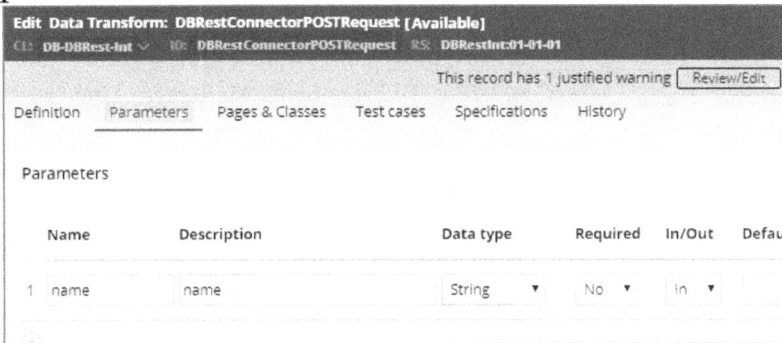

	Name	Description	Data type	Required	In/Out	Defaul
1	name	name	String ▾	No ▾	In ▾	

Edit Data Transform: DBRestConnectorPOSTRequest [Available]
CL: DB-DBRest-Int ∨   ID: DBRestConnectorPOSTRequest   RS: DBRestInt:01-01-01

This record has 1 justified warning [Review/Edit]

Definition Parameters Pages & Classes Test cases Specifications History

Parameters

Figure 78: Defining the Parameters for the Request Data Transform

Definition Tab

In the definition tab, we just need to do 2 steps:
1) Set the *"name"* to be the parameter being passed in
2) Convert the request page containing the *"name"* parameter to *"Param.JSON"*

The following shows the completed form:

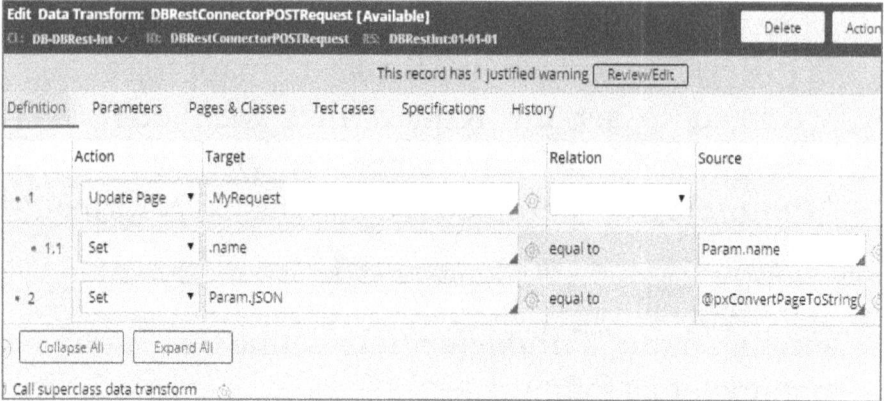

Figure 79: Preparing the Request JSON for the Test Datapage

> *Note:* The function that is called in the 2nd line is as follows:
> **@pxConvertPageToString(tools, .MyRequest, "json").**

> *Note:* Recall that the ".*MyRequest*" was defined earlier as a 'member variable' of the "DB-DBRest-Int" class? That is why we could use that temporarily for data manipulation and using it for converting the information to "**Param.JSON**" for sending.

Response Mapping Configuration

Back in the "**D_DBRestConnectorPOST**" *datapage*, click on the icon on the right of the "*Response Data Transform*" field, this will create the given rule for you.

> *Note:* The name entered above is "**DBRestConnectorPOSTResponse**".

> **Note:** By default, Pega creates some boilerplate codes for you. These include a "**Datasource**" page (as defined in the **Parameters** tab, that contains the returned info, as well as some codes to show you how to initiate a mapping. It also contains some error handling templates.
> As we are using "**Param.JSON**", we do not need to use the "**Datasource**" page. For the error handling, we will discuss it in the Master Beaver Version.

Definition Tab

The following shows the mapping in the response data transform:

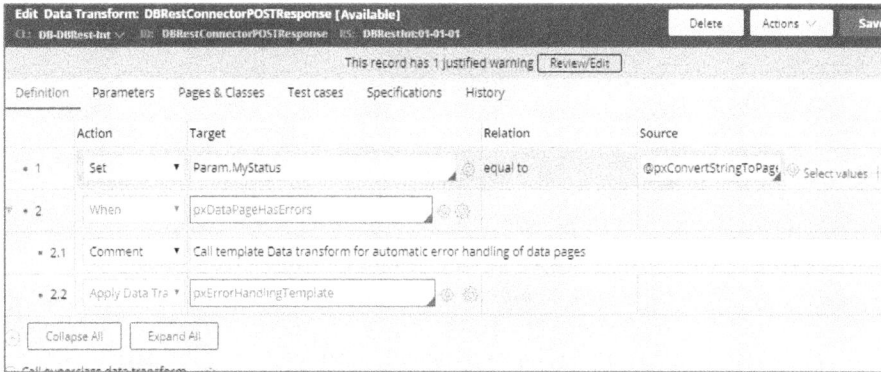

Figure 80: Preparing the Response JSON for the Test Datapage

Basically there is only 1 step, which is as follows:

```
@pxConvertStringToPage(tools, .MyResponse, Param.JSON,"json")
```

This line basically converts the "*Param.JSON*" that is passed to us from the REST service, into the "*.MyResponse*" page.

> **Note:** The Step 2 above is actually disabled by default. Again, we will talk about that in the Master Beaver Version later.

Running the Datapage

OK, that is all that is required! Ensure that you have saved all the rules, and let's do a test now!

Back in the *"D_DBRestConnectorPOST"* *datapage*, click on *"Actions"*, followed by the *"Run"* menu item.

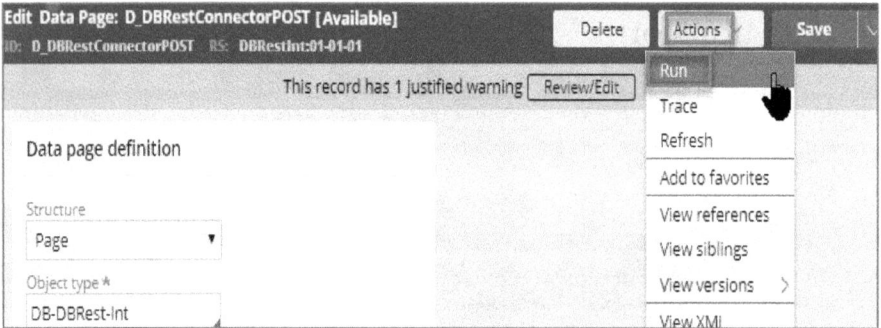

Figure 81: Invoking the REST Testing Datapage

In the popup dialog box, enter *"Debunkum Beaver :-)"*, and then click the *"Run"* button.

In the output, expand the *"MyResponse"* element and you will see that the output *"WelcomeMsg"* and the *"YourName"* are populated accordingly!

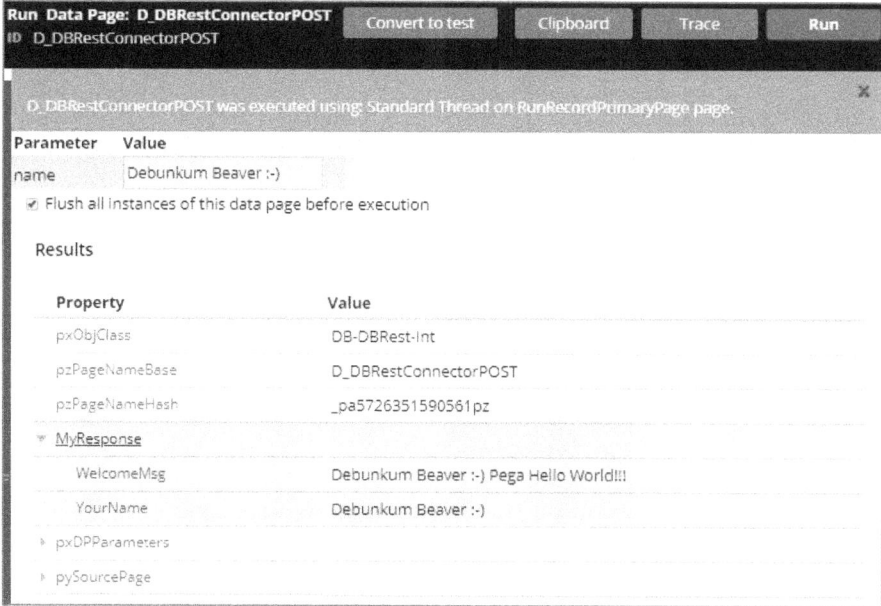

Figure 82: Output from the Testing of REST Service Using Datapage

Wow, it is cool and simple, isn't it? 😎

In the Master Beaver Version, we will drill into more details!

Part 3: Further Discussions (Master Beaver Version ONLY)

[This How-to Version has outlines ONLY]

Introduction to Master Beaver Version

In this section, I will touch on some discussions on REST itself. At the same time, I will go through some of the changes to the earlier rules, so that you can better understand why I had done what I did.

For a start, I will talk about the various method, not as an academic discussion, but rather from a practical standpoint.

After that, I will demonstrate some changes to the REST service, to make it much more reliable.

Note: For Master Beaver Version, I will skip some details such as the step-by-step creation of the rules, etc. I would expect that you are familiar with those, either from your working experience or from the How-to Version above. Nevertheless, for the screenshots, I will still provide you with the name and class that I used so that it is easier for you to follow through.

Discussion on the Various REST Methods

In this chapter, we will talk about the various REST method: GET, POST, PUT, DELETE, as well as the PATCH method (Pega 8.x only).

> Q *Note: Just a reminder: The discussion points about various methods mentioned here are not meant for academic definition; rather, it is simplified a lot to make it easier to understand and implement it in Pega. If you want the definition, Internet is your source.*

Get Method

> Q *Note: If you inspect some URLs, you might notice the "?" symbol. This indicates the starting of the name-value pair of parameters. Each name-value pair is then separated by the "&" symbol. For example:*
> *http://www.DebunkumBeaver.com/find?**LookFor=Book&TheItem=CLSAGuide***
>
> *In the above, Pega will create the parameters with the following values:*
> *Param.LookFor → Book*
> *Param.TheItem → CLSAGuide*

Note: Passing parameters through the URL can also be accomplished using "sub-path" of the URL. For example, in the following URLs:
http://www.DebunkumBeaver.com/**Book/CLSAGuide**
http://www.DebunkumBeaver.com/**Post/Latest**

I can define that the 1st part (Book/Post) to be what the requestor is looking for, while the 2nd part to be the details of the item. In such a case, I can instruct Pega to return the 1st part as Param.LookFor, while the 2nd part as Param.TheItem.

In the 1st example, Pega will pass me Param.LookFor=Book; while Param.TheItem=CLSAGuide.

Within the activity code, I can then use those 2 parameters to formulate my queries for the Report Definition, etc.

Note: CGI stands for "Common Gateway Interface". In the early days of the Internet, request sent to a web server are often passed to a program typically written in C language for more complex processing. The C program typically calls the "getenv()" function to get the parameters, perform the necessary actions, and 'print' the response as HTML code back through the standard output, e.g. stdout, etc.

Don't worry about this, this has nothing to do with Pega!

POST Method

Note: Of course, using POST, you can still send parameters via the URL or the query string too. However, since you could pass the parameters in the request body itself, most implementations may not use the URL or the query string. But again, these all depend on the relevant design.

Note: Instead of JSON, you can also send and receive XML. Basically, whether it is SOAP or REST, ultimately, it is still leveraging on HTTP protocol. Just like how you use your browser, you enter a URL (starting with "http"), it then returns you a bunch of text (HTML codes).

In the case of REST, you just define the standard, it then returns you either JSON or XML formatted text string. There is really no magic to it, just some standard definition of the messages!

Note: Many years ago (before 1998), where XML was not even defined, many people, including myself had already implemented such request and response stuff. At that time, I created a client program using MS Visual C++, which communicated with the server through http url data passing. On the server side, I was using ColdFusion (not sure if you are old enough to know that). The communication protocol was simple, I passed the data through URL (GET Method), and the ColdFusion would query the database and return the result using the "name-value" format. Example:
CustomerLevel=Gold
TotalSpent=5000

As you can see, the basic is very simple. So, don't confuse yourself with the details, in fact, when you are using tools such as Pega, your life had just become much easier!

PUT Method

Note: The difference between POST and PUT is that PUT requests are idempotent. That is, calling the same PUT request multiple times will always produce the same result. In contrast, calling a POST request repeatedly have the side effects of creating the same resource multiple times.

Note: I have seen some material stating that POST is for creating resources while PUT is for updating resources, so just take note.

DELETE Method

PATCH Method

Enough Confusion? Here Is More

Q *Note:* I have come across articles, which state that if you have an object with properties of [ID], [Name], [Telephone], [Address], and if you need to update just the [ID] and [Address], using PUT will 'wipe' out the [Name] and [Telephone] values of that record, while a PATCH will be 'smart' enough to update only those relevant fields while retaining those that are not affected.

This statement may not be technically correct in Pega's perspective, therefore, in actual implementation, always requests for samples and scenario on the expectation before you implement it. BTW, if you are not using Pega 8.x, there is no PATCH method.

Q *Note:* To be a technical leader, such as Pega CLSA, you are expected to know all these (even though these are not covered in the Pega Academy training). In particular, given some implementation requirements, you must be able to architect and explain how to use the various methods to achieve the requirements!

Implementing Error Handling

In our earlier codes, we had simply returned "200" (success) for all situation. However, in an actual project implementation, this approach is not acceptable.

At the very least, you should always provide at least the "200" (for success) and "500" (for failure).

Let's go back to the earlier REST service. Since the GET method example that we did earlier did not take in any parameters and basically just return a hard-coded message, it would be more difficult to use that as an example to demonstrate the different error code.

Therefore, we shall modify the POST method such that it could conditionally return either "200" or "500", based upon some inputs of ours.

Changes to the Service REST

Method Tab

Figure 83: Updating REST Service Status Code to Use Param.StatusCode

Service Activity

Step 1: (No changes)

Figure 84: Implemented Error Handling - Step 1 of POST Activity

Step 2: (Added the StatusCode 500 and "Jump" Condition)

Figure 85: Implemented Error Handling - Step 2 of POST Activity

Figure 86: Step 2 of POST Activity – Settings for the Jump Conditions

⚠ **Warning:** *You would not be able to define the "Jump" because the "RET" label is not defined yet! It shall be defined in Step 4! So please take note of this and come back to edit it after you have implemented Step 4!*

Note: *In activity step, the "When" is being testing before the step, so as to decide if you are going to run that step. The "Jump" will only be tested if that step had been run!*

Since our logic is that if this step is run (i.e. there is error), we would want to skip the Step 3 (which is setting the "WelcomeMsg"). Therefore, the "Jump" condition was set as "Always", which means that if this step is run, I would always want to skip the Step 3 by jumping to the step marked with the "RET" label.

Note: *The "Jump" setting is available at the right side of every activity step. This allows you to make a decision on what to do next based on the outcome of the given step.*

Note: *The "Always" When rule is an OOTB When rule, which always evaluated to true. The opposite of it is "Never", which never evaluate to true! [Quite a nice naming convention!]*

Step 3: (Added the StatusCode of 200)

Figure 87: Implemented Error Handling - Step 3 of POST Activity

Step 4: (Added the "RET" label)
Figure 88: Implemented Error Handling - Step 4 of POST Activity

Testing the REST POST Method Again
Figure 89: Launching the OOTB Test REST Service Tool

Figure 90: Execute the REST POST With Empty Input for Error Testing

Figure 91: Sample Error Output With StatusCode of 500

Figure 92: Execute the REST POST With Earlier Valid Input

Figure 93: Sample Success Output With StatusCode of 200

Note: *The above demonstrated how to implement error handling and setting the status code, however, the actual status code would depend on your specific scenario.*

Check for Errors from Datapage

In the earlier chapters, we had created a datapage to encapsulate the REST service call. In this chapter we will discuss how to check for errors returned from the datapage.

In the earlier error testing, we had intentionally entered some invalid JSON, such as an empty one. However, in the case of the datapage, even if we give it an empty name, internally, the Request Data Transform would still make it valid.

Simulating Errors

Figure 94: Entering Invalid Endpoint for Error Testing

> **Note:** *In the above, we had simulated errors by changing the "**Endpoint URL**" to an invalid one. However, you should know that by doing the above, it will not hit the REST service that we had created, thus, it is not possible to handle any such error there!*

Figure 95: Error In Datapage - Presence of pyErrorPage

Note: As a best practice, after you invoked a datapage, you MUST always check for the existence of the "**pyErrorPage**" (such as using the function "**@PageExists**". If it is present, you should get the relevant error message and notify the caller.

Note: Never assign property values directly to any datapage! This is because you should check for any error first! Also, by assigning values directly to the datapage, you are actually invoking the same datapage multiple times, this is not necessary and should be avoided!

Invoke Datapage Using Data Transform

Since the invoked datapage takes in a *"name"* parameter, we shall also define this DT to take in the same parameter. To do that, just define it in the Parameters tab.

Parameters tab

Figure 96: Adding the "name" Parameter

Pages & Classes tab

Figure 97: Defining a Temp Page to Invoke Datapage

> **Note:** *I like to simply add a "Temp" in front of the temp page used for invoking the datapage, this is easy for me to remember too! It is also best to define it as the same type as the actual datapage for simplicity.*

Definition tab

Figure 98: Invoking a Datapage Using Data Transform

If you would like to copy-and-paste, these are the actual codes:

Step 1:

Step 2:

Step 3:

Step 4:

💡 **Note:** *".pyNote" are often used for quick testing or some non-important stuff. However, some developers used that as a quick-fix for some codes. Therefore, you should be careful when trying to use this variable.*

Running the Data Transform

Happy Path Testing

> *Figure 99: Running a Data Transform*

⚠️ **Warning:** *Make sure you have cleared the earlier error in the previous chapter by clearing the value in the "**Endpoint URL**" field before you try this happy path scenario.*

Figure 100: Invoke REST Service Through Data Transform Using Datapage

Figure 101: DT Successfully Returned the Intended Results

Failure Scenario

> *Figure 102: Simulating Error for REST Invocation*

Figure 103: DT Returned the Corresponding Error Messages

Invoke Datapage Using Activity

For simplicity and atomicity, let's create this activity in "*DB-DBRest-Int*" class.

Q *Note: Usually, rules for testing purposes are saved in a separate ruleset (e.g. TestRuleset), such that you do not deploy it to production. There are developers who are so strict that they do not allow it in SIT, UAT. I feel that this is bunkum, and it is very ignorant to attempt to follow guidelines so blindly that ended up creating more problems downstream.*
In a real-world scenario, it really makes a lot of sense to have some 'pinging' rules to test workability of specific points. Thus, for me, I would still prefer to deploy such 'ping-test' rules in SIT and UAT –provided it only does 'point-testing' and does not change any underlying data.

Q *Note: Test ruleset should be set as production ruleset for a specific group (e..g administrators), not in the application ruleset in order to prevent it from accidentally deployed to production. However, I noticed that if you do not put it into the application ruleset, it does not appear in the App Explorer, which I felt is quite painful and non-intuitive.*

Q *Note: It is always a good programming practice to create some form of parallelism in the coding, so as to make it easier for others to understand how to perform the same thing using another rule. This is what I am trying to achieve here!*

> **Note:** *Implementing using Pega is easy, but to implement it in such a way that is easy to understand and easy to modify, that is what separate a good Pega Developer from a mediocre one. Unfortunately, more often than not, I often see messy codes around.* ☹

Parameters tab

Figure 104: Parameters Tab of Activity That Invokes the Datapage

Pages & Classes tab

Figure 105: Pages & Classes Tab of Activity That Invokes the Datapage

Definition tab

Step 1:

Figure 106: Step 1 of InvokeRestConnectorPOST Activity

Step 2:

Figure 107: Step 2 of InvokeRestConnectorPOST Activity

Figure 108: When Condition: Step 2 of InvokeRestConnectorPOST Activity

> ⚠ **Warning:** *You would not be able to complete the "**When**" condition now because the "ELSE" label is not defined yet! It shall be defined in Step 4! So, complete this later.*

Figure 109: Jump Condition: Step 2 of InvokeRestConnectorPOST Activity

> **Note:** *When you have a "**Always**" When condition, it is always better to enter the same values for both the "**if true**" and "**if false**". This will make it easier to understand.*

Step 3:

Figure 110: Step 3 of InvokeRestConnectorPOST Activity

Step 4:

Figure 111: Step 4 of InvokeRestConnectorPOST Activity

Running the Activity

Figure 112: Invoking the Actions->Run of Activity

💡 **Note:** *Since in our testing in the previous chapter (using data transform), we had intentionally created an error by setting the "**Endpoint URL**" as "**ERRORURL**" (which is still set as such), let's leverage on that and test the Failure Scenario first!*

Failure Scenario

Figure 113: Entering the "name" to Test for Failure Scenario

Figure 114: Success Message When Running Activity

Figure 115: Output from Activity in RunRecordPrimaryPage

Happy Path Testing

Figure 116: D_DBRestConnectorPOST With the Endpoint URL Cleared Off

Figure 117: Success Message When Running Activity With No Content

Figure 118: Successful Message from REST Service Invoked From Activity

Should I Enable Run On Data Page Option?

Another interesting thing you may have noticed is the *"Run on data page"* option, which you could tick to enable it. So, should you enable it?

> **Note:** This *"Run on data page"* was not available in earlier versions, it seems to be added since Pega 7.3.

Figure 119: "Run on data page" Option

Figure 120: "Create" Icon – Generates a Default Response Data Transform

Generated Response Data Transform

Figure 121: Generated Data Transform ("Run on data page" Unticked)

Figure 122: Generated Data Transform ("Run on data page" Ticked)

Differences in the Mapping Logic

Figure 123: DataSource Page Generated By Pega

> **Note:** The *"Class"* of your *"DataSource"* will be different, depending on how your datapage was being defined.

Differences in the Datapage Output

Figure 124: Datapage Executed Without The "Run on data page" Option

Figure 125: Datapage Executed With The "Run on data page" Option

> 💡 **Tip:** *Hey! By changing the "**Run on data page**", I should be showing you the changes in the mapping of the response data transform since I would then need to map from "**DataSource**" instead, isn't it?*
>
> *Well, actually... I don't have to!!! 😎 This is because I had already 'elevated' myself out of all these messes by using the "**Param.JSON**" and NOT relying on the "**Primary**" for mapping!*
>
> *These are the kind of things that you will <u>NEITHER</u> learn from Pega Academy <u>NOR</u> from any other LSAs. This requires not just Pega technical expertise (CLSA), but also the desire to explore better implementation techniques that would work for all cases. Most importantly, the willingness and ability to share the knowledge! Thus, the purpose of me writing the Debunkum Beaver Series!* ✌️

Leveraging OOTB Error Handling

In the generated response data transform of the datapage, you would have noticed that there are some error handling codes that Pega had generated for you.

Figure 126: Generated Error Handling, Initially Disabled

💡 **Note:** *Let's create the same error by setting the endpoint to "ERRORURL". You can refer to the earlier chapters on the details to perform this setting.*

Without Error Handling

Figure 127: Unhandled Error Message When Running Datapage

Figure 128: Unhandled Error Message Showing in Clipboard Page

💡 **Note:** *As we are running via "Run" button in Designer Studio, the "Standard" clipboard was used.*

Adding Error Handling

Enable the block of *"When pxDataPageHasErrors"*

Figure 129: Enabling Codes in Data Transform

Copy the default *"pxErrorHandlingTemplate"*

Figure 130: Performing a Save-As for the Default Error Template

Figure 131: Our New Error Template

Enable 2 lines of codes

Figure 132: Enable 2 Lines of Code in the Error Handling Template

> **Note:** Strictly speaking, "px" rules from Pega are those that we <u>should</u> <u>not</u> modify. However, if you inspect the context and purpose of this *"<u>px</u>ErrorHandlingTemplate"*, and the fact that all the steps are disabled initially, it clearly depicted the need to modify it, else, it would be totally useless!!! Therefore, my 'guess' is that this could be a 'naming bug'! In other words, given the purpose of this rule, it should have been named *"<u>py</u>ErrorHandlingTemplate"* and also should not have been set as *"[Final]"*. This would then indicate that developers are expected to enable it and do their own configurations.

Testing With Error Handling

Figure 133: Datapage Output With Error Handling

Figure 134: Clipboard page Output With Error Handling

> **Note:** Whether the error is marked as RED or not, it may not really matter. However, personally, I prefer to keep things clean. Even in Java programming, I would try my best NOT to have any stack trace dump in the log file! By doing so, not only would it be easier for me to scan the log files for issues, I also minimised the overall log file size!

Using Actual Classes

In the earlier chapters, I had used the "$ANY" instead of the actual class name. It is always a good practice to use actual class name so that Pega could help you detect other forms of errors (such as typo errors) during development.

At the beginning of development, most of the properties are often not finalised (this is especially true when doing new service interfaces). It would be a big hassle trying to define all of those at the beginning of the development, and then going around updating all those along the way!

In this chapter, we will assume that the properties are now finalised, and we are going to update our rules accordingly.

> Q **Note:** For simplicity and record purposes, I am not going to change the current code, instead, I will simulate the changes in the PUT Method. By doing so, we will have 2 copies of codes that we could review and compare later!

Page Definition To Be Replaced

Figure 135: MyRequest As Page Property Of $ANY

Figure 136: MyResponse As Page Property Of $ANY

Ω
Note: The "MyRequest" in Figure 135 and "MyResponse" in Figure 136 are both properties of type "Single Page", and their Page Type is "$ANY". Those 2 properties are used in our earlier examples for us to store values.

Now, instead of using the "$ANY" Page Type, we are going to define REAL classes (i.e. some REAL Page Type), that would contain the actual properties that we need for the "Single Page" for our new properties. This REAL classes, shall be named as follows:
For Request: "DB-DBRest-Int-MyRequest"
For Response: "DB-DBRest-Int-MyResponse"

Creating The New Classes

Ω
Note: If you are not using this method to create classes but decided to type in the full class name all by yourself, beware of the uppercase/lowercase for all the parent classes! I have seen applications with hyphenated class name, which was the result of typing in the wrong parent classes, it was horrific!

Figure 137: Navigation To Create a New Class

Ω
Note: Noticed that I do not need to browse through the classes to find the "DB-DBRest-Int" class? This is because I had pinned those classes, which is indicated by the "Pinned classes" label as shown above.

Figure 138: Create Class dialog box

Figure 139: The Completed "MyRequest" Class

Ω
Note: At a minimum, you need to specify the "Created in version", as well as fill in the "Description" and the "Usage" fields in the History tab.

Note: Since we are using this class as a data structure, not for storing data, we just need to set it as "Abstract". The same applies for the MyResponse class.

Figure 140: The Completed "MyResponse" Class

Tip: An easier way to create the "MyResponse" class is to perform a "Save As" of the earlier "MyRequest" class.

Defining Properties for MyRequest

Figure 141: Navigating the Menu Item To Create Property

Figure 142: Created "name" Property for the MyRequest Class

Note: In the earlier rules, we had used the property "name", which is in lowercase. Therefore, to maintain the same consistency, remember to change the identifier manually to reflect this. By default, Pega would generate it as "Name" instead. The same applies to the "errorMessage" in the "MyResponse" class below.

Defining Properties for MyResponse

Figure 143: Created " Status" Property for the MyResponse Class

Figure 144: Created "errorMessage" Property for the MyResponse Class

Figure 145: Created "WelcomeMsg" Property for the MyResponse Class

Figure 146: Created "YourName" Property for the MyResponse Class

Viewing the Properties In the Explorer

Figure 147: Created Properties Viewed In App Explorer

Using the New Page Definition

147

Create MyNewRequest Property

Figure 148: The MyNewRequest Property

Create MyNewResponse Property

Figure 149: The MyNewResponse Property

Viewing the New Properties In the Explorer

Figure 150: MyNewRequest and MyNewResponse Properties

> ♀ *Note:* Do not be confused on the *"MyNewRequest"* & *"MyNewResponse"* properties with the *"name"*, *"Status"*, etc. properties. The *"name"*, *"Status"*, etc. are simple text properties of the class: "DB-DBRest-Int-MyRequest" & "DB-DBRest-Int-MyResponse". On the other hand, the *"MyNewRequest"* & *"MyNewResponse"* properties are properties of the *"DB-DBRest-Int"*, which are both Page properties of type *"DB-DBRest-Int-MyRequest"* & *"DB-DBRest-Int-MyResponse"*.

> ♀ *Note:* As you are on your way to be a Master Beaver, I will start to skip the actual rule creation steps and jump straight into the created rules. This will save some time for all of us. If you still need guidance, please feel free to refer to earlier chapters / books for the step-by-step guidance.

Implementing the PUT Method

> ♀ *Note:* Just another reminder again, we are doing the PUT method out of simplicity and convenience. If you are required to provide a RESTful service, please read the earlier chapters on some rules that you would need to follow.

Figure 151: Newly Created DoDBTestPUT Activity

Update the DoDBTestPUT By Searching

Figure 152: Searching for Text in Rule

Figure 153: Updated DoDBTestPUT Activity

Update the Service REST

Figure 154: Settings for the PUT Method

Figure 155: Request Tab Settings for the PUT Method

Figure 156: Response Tab Settings for the PUT Method

Testing the PUT Method

Figure 157: Invoking the PUT Method

Figure 158: Output from the Testing of the PUT Method

Problem with pxObjClass

All are well and good!!! **EXCEPT** the following!!!

Response Parameter Values

DATA TYPE   VALUE

java.lang.String   { "pxObjClass":"DB-DBRest-Int-MyResponse","WelcomeMsg":"Debunkum Beaver Pega Hello World!!!","YourName":"Debunkum Beaver" }

Figure 159: Undesirable "pxObjClass" Output in the Response

> 💡 **Note:** This is what I had been trying to state again and again. Having a Pega PSA/LSA with many years of experiences does not necessarily mean you will get better output. The version in which the person was certified in, and how updated he is with newer Pega version are very critical! Most importantly, the willingness to listen and accept ideas that is conflicting with his 'World-of-Truth'.

> 💡 **Note:** Being up-to-date in the latest version of Pega does not guarantee the ability to apply new features to solve real-world issues, it takes an innovative mind and character to achieve that. As a technical lead, you should always aim to elevate yourself beyond pure product features.

Removing pxObjClass

In a proper implementation, there is always the painful *"pxObjClass"* that gets populated in the response. It was impossible to remove them in earlier versions of Pega, until now.

Definition Tab
Settings Tab
Testing the Removal

Go back to the Service REST and click the *"Run"*. In the opened dialog, click on the *"Execute"* button (as what we did in *"Figure 158: Output from the Testing of the PUT Method"*).

Take a look at the new output, you will no longer have the *".pxObjClass"*!!!

Simulation Results for REST Service DBRestPackage.v1.dbtest42f83c61e9ce0d9555ddd55

Overall Result

Success

List of Steps

STEP	RESULT
Lookup Service Properties	Not Attempted
Initialize Requestor	Not Attempted
Perform Authentication	Not Attempted
Initialize Primary Page	Success
Map Inbound Data	Success
Invoke Service Activity	Success
Determine Response Type	Success
Map Outbound Data	Success

Response Header Values

HEADER	VALUE
HTTP Status code	200

Response Parameter Values

DATA TYPE	VALUE
java.lang.String	{"YourName":"Debunkum Beaver","WelcomeMsg":"Debunkum Beaver Pega Hello World!!!"}

Figure 160: New REST Response Without the "pxObjClass"

Cool and simple, isn't it?

So far, we had been doing testing within Pega. In the next chapter, let's explore using external tool to test our REST service!

Testing Using External Tool – Postman

Since Pega already provided us with a tool to test our REST service, why should we even bother to use any external tool?

Why Bother Using an External Tool?

Using Postman

Figure 161: Initial Postman Screen

Figure 162: Getting the Endpoint URL of the REST Service

Figure 163: Entering the Service URL in Postman

Invoking Via "GET" Method

Figure 164: Invoking Our REST Service Using "GET" Method

Q **Note:** Don't be fooled by the "200 OK" status! In our service for the "GET" method, we had hardcoded the response as "200"!

Invoking Via "*POST*" Method

Figure 165: Testing the Error Scenario Using Postman

Figure 166: Entering Inputs for the "POST" Method

Figure 167: Invoking Our REST Service Using "POST" Method

Note: *If you are not able to see the output, you may need to drag the window upwards (see the black double arrows pointing both up-and-down in the middle of the diagram above).*

Adding Security to REST Service

Remember that initially, we had turned off the security? It is always a good practice to ensure that there is some form of authentication, so let's turn it back on!

Turning On REST Service Security

Figure 168: Enabling Authentication in REST Service Package

💡 **Note:** *Just a reminder, you should define a specific "**Service access group**" for the purpose of service package, not the typical users/developers type of access group. The worst case is using the "**Administrators**" as shown above!*

💡 **Tip:** *Notice the "**Pooling**" tab? If you go to that tab, you will see configurations such as "**Maximum active requestors**", "**Maximum wait (in seconds)**", etc.*
What this means is that you would need to decide how many services, such as Service REST, to bundle into each service package. If you have multiple REST Services that has huge number of concurrencies, you would need to configure this accordingly!

Figure 169: Entering Authentication Info In Postman

💡 **Note:** *It is a best practice to use a functional user just for the purpose of service invocation, not your actual Designer Studio user.*
Figure 170: Postman Giving TLS/SSL Required Error

Figure 171: Untick the "Require TLS/SSL for REST services in this package"

💡 **Note:** *When you use "**Basic**" authentication type, username and password are passed as clear text, which is not secured, thus Pega has this automatic check and you will also get a corresponding Guardrail warning message, stating: "**Use of TLS/SSL is strongly recommended for services using Basic Authentication.**". "TLS/SSL" is a separate topic by itself, and it is out of scope for this book. For now, we shall just justify the warning.*

Figure 172: Using Postman with Basic Authentication

Conclusion

Congratulation! You have completed the _REST Service and REST Connector Pega How-to Guide_! You are now ready to do real-world implementation!

In this How-to Guide, I had showed you how to use Pega to create a REST Service, as well as a REST Connector to consume the service.

I had implemented various methods, such as _"GET"_, _"POST"_, _"PUT"_, as well as talked about the _"DELETE"_ and the _"PATCH"_ methods.

I had demonstrated how to create the REST service without defining the actual data structure and the motivation for taking this approach during development.

> **Note:** *For simplicity, I had created all my rules under the "**Int**" class. In general, case related rules should be under "**Work**" class, data related rules should be under "**Data**" class.*
>
> *In other words, if you have properties that are specific to the integration interfaces, those should be in "**Int**" class. Datapages and its corresponding data sources should be under the "**Data**" class. Whether there are exceptions, that is beside the point, but in general, you need to know these best practices.*

In the ***Master Beaver Version***, I started off with a high-level discussion on the various REST methods, followed by implementing error handling for the REST Service.

I had also demonstrated invoking a datapage via data transform and activity and showed how to implement error handling for datapage.

After that, I had also discussed and demonstrated the differences of implementing the datapage with the option ***"Run on data page"*** ticked and how it could affect your data mapping and error handlings.

Following that, I also showed how to remove the ***"pxObjClass"*** that was returned by Pega by default.

In closing, I had demonstrated invoking our Pega REST Service using external tools, such as *Postman*, as well as explained why it is critical to use external tools for testing in a real-world project implementation.

Apart from that, I had also enabled the security in our REST service and updated *Postman* with the relevant login information to authenticate and retrieve the response.

In this book, I had covered the core complexities of the Pega REST Service and REST Connector, by using the *"Hello World"* as an example.

By now, you should realise that although the book uses *"Hello World"*, which may seem very simple, but in fact, you now have the necessary capabilities and knowledge to implement a real-world *REST Service and REST Connector* application!

The next thing that you need to do to extend your actual application, would basically be defining more properties for the request and response, as well as to use the request properties, to do querying/processing so as to return the output as the JSON response!

Note: *Querying / Processing is a separate topic that I will cover in the future.*

If you look back at what you had learnt, I am sure you will realise that there are a lot of knowledge that you would NEVER be able to learn from Pega Academy or even from senior LSA/PSA.

This is because the above are not purely technical knowledge, but also encompassed my personal experiences as well as my character. Personally, when I implement a feature and felt any awkwardness in it, I will always try to do it in a different way to make the implementation smoother and easier to explain and extend.

On top of that, I always prefer to use a single method, rather than different methods of achieving the same thing.

When there are multiple methods, each would typically have its own restrictions, and it would be too difficult for me to remember when to use which, and difficult to pass the knowledge around!

It is my hope that you always aim to elevate yourself beyond pure product features, leveraging on an innovative and open mind to deliver maximum values to your customers.

Last but not least, there are other publications from the *"Debunkum Beaver series"*, remember to take a look at those too!

I have many other topics to write, but if you have anything in particular, just drop me a note. If that topic is popular, I will try to do that first!

Other Books in the Collections

Debunkum Beaver Pega CLSA Guide:
Preparing for Pega CLSA 7.3/7.4
Certification (Book 1)

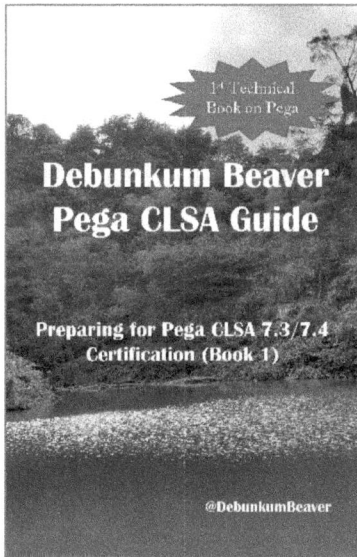

ISBN: 9789811703102
ISBN: 9781796641936

Debunkum Beaver Pega How-to Guide: Installing and Setting Up AES

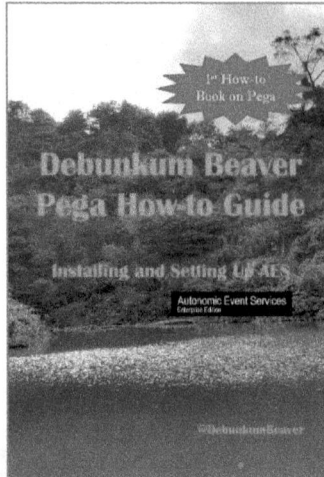

ISBN: 9789811413599

Watch out for more releases at:

URL: https://www.DebunkumBeaver.com

Twitter: https://twitter.com/DebunkumBeaver